My Life Circle, Squared

RICHARD ODEN

These are some of the motivational quotes found with in this book, please use these as I have, and let them help you become a better person! Thank you so much for your purchase and support!" May God bless you and keep you!

1. "Experience is not what happens to you but what you do with what happens to you"
2. "I will do the things that you will not in order to continue to do the things you cannot"
3. "Dare to change those around you not to change into those around you"
4. "Someday never comes, what does come is Monday through Friday plus Saturday and Sunday"
5. "You stress you fray, I stress I pray!"

ISBN 978-1-63525-562-1 (Paperback)
ISBN 978-1-63525-564-5 (Hard Cover)
ISBN 978-1-63525-563-8 (Digital)

Christian Faith Publishing, Inc.
296 Chestnut Street
Meadville, PA 16335
www.christianfaithpublishing.com

Printed in the United States of America

Dedication

First and foremost, I would like to dedicate this book to my parents, Gerry and Debbie Oden: without you giving my sister and me something we so desperately wanted and needed, this book and my story would not have been possible. You had four of your own children, one happy family, and so many others would have been content with that. Because of your compassionate, loving hearts, you guys did what so many wouldn't, and for that I am truly thankful. I'm sure my kids, your grandkids, will learn to be truly thankful for it as well!

I would like to dedicate this book to the men and women with whom I served in Bagram, Afghanistan, especially cell two, with the 187th Fighter Wing. I dedicate this book to all veterans who have served honorably everywhere—past, present, and future—and their families. Because of you, my passion to serve my country led me to enlist when I was 28 years old. Thank you and your families for your service to our great county!

I would like to dedicate this book to *you*. *You* know who *you* are; *you* are the ones who will heed my call to action, whether it be to take that leap of faith with God and become foster/adoptive parents or, for those who are not cut out for that, to serve those who are! If *you* are that individual or family who has decided to support our military and their families, to go the extra mile with that support, I dedicate this book to *you*! One more thing—if you used this book as a stepping stone to find and know God, I am truly honored, and I dedicate this book to *you* as well!

Lastly, I want to dedicate this book to my sweet wife, Brittany! Babe, you have a heart of gold, and many people can get a glimpse of God's heart because of yours. I have loved you since middle school, and I love you more than ever today; thank you for joining me on my mission to pay this forward and for letting me serve my country! 143!

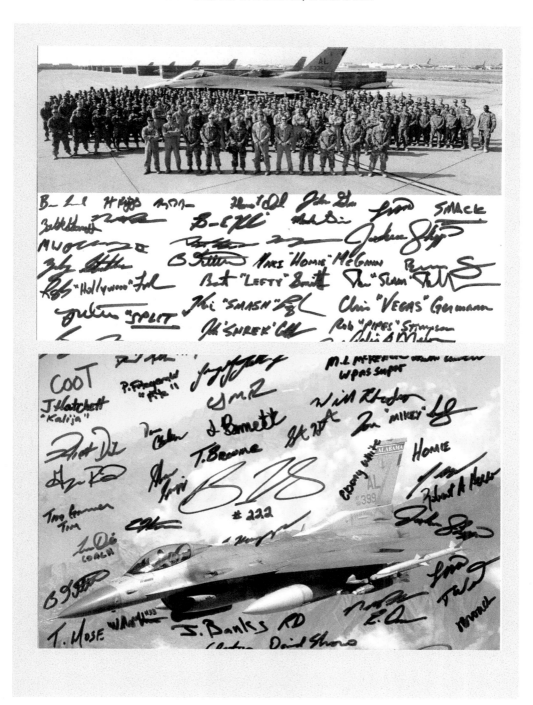

CHAPTER 1

My Beginnings

First Corinthians 15:10 reads, "But by the grace of God I am what I am, and His grace toward me was not in vain; but I labored more abundantly than they all, yet not I, but the grace of God which was with me."[1].

Throughout this book I will try to guide the reader through three things simultaneously; first, my biography, second, different people's perspectives that have been in my life; and third, what is happening in real time while I'm writing this book—somewhat like a book within a book within a book, if you will. Also, throughout this book I will chime in and out of the actual events happening on my deployment to Afghanistan, where I wrote most of this book, to help the reader I will make the text gray.

As a little boy I would often ask God why he put me in foster care. I would ask why I couldn't have a normal life like some of the other kids I knew—a life that had, what we foster kids refer to as, our real mom and dad. Throughout my life God has answered these questions time and again. My prayer is that He blesses me with the wisdom, courage, strength, and words to show you and the world the providence of Him and His will in my life. I know beyond a

---

[1]   All Scriptures are taken from the New King James Version®. Copyright© 1982 by Thomas Nelson, Inc. Used by permission. All rights reserved.

shadow of a doubt that He put me in this situation so one day I could, indeed, inspire, encourage, motivate, and minister to others.

Jeremiah 29:11 reads, "For I know the thoughts that I think toward you, says the Lord, thoughts of peace and not of evil, to give you **a future and a hope**."

I was born in West Covina, California (Los Angeles County), at Queen of the Valley Hospital on May 31, 1982, at 4:30 in the afternoon. My full name was Richard Sundown Robert Paul Golec. I know your first question; I hear it all the time: Sundown? I have no idea. I did google what time the sun sets in Southern California in May but it wasn't anywhere close to 4:34 PM. It was more like 8:30 PM. Maybe one day my biologicals will read this book and we will find one another and I'll get back with you. Anyway, I digress. My first memories are of us living in a house in a state that I think was in the northwest. I had a mom, dad, an older brother, older sister, then me, then Laura Machelle Elizabeth Ann Golec and last there was the baby Michael. I don't know what his full name was because we were told he died of crib death. From these memories I thought for a short time that I, in fact, did have a normal kid's life. But that turned out to be the calm before the storm. About the time that Michael died my father just took off, no good-bye or anything—he just left. I think or assume that his leaving might have had to do with the baby's death but I really think I am giving him the benefit of the doubt. I haven't seen the man since. I don't remember how old I was when he left. I know I couldn't have been very old because these are some of the first memories I can remember, if that makes any sense. I do know I had to be just a little thing, and now I am thirty-one.

Throughout this book I want you, my readers, to know where I was when I was writing it. I don't know, I guess I thought it would be neat for you to see what was going on in actual time in my world. I began this book on one of my drill weekends. The date is October 5, 2013, at 10:05 in the morning. I proudly serve in the 187th Fighter

Wing as a crew chief on the F-16 fighter jet, the Fighting Falcons, descendants of the Tuskegee Airmen, Red Tails. It is also the descendent unit in which the 43rd president of the United States, George W. Bush, served. The unit is now based out of Dannelly Field in Montgomery, Alabama. The reason I have some time to start this book now is that we are in the middle of a government shutdown. We were told all units' drills across the country were cancelled except for ours and two others. Why ours, you might ask. It has a lot to do with the fact that we are scheduled to deploy to Bagram, Afghanistan, in April of 2014. They grounded our jets and had us come in to get caught up on paper and computer work that we need to deploy. Anyways, my dad took off. The next memories I have are of me with my mom, her boyfriend, and my siblings traveling in a covered pickup truck. In that truck, we ate and slept a lot of the time. Sometimes we would get bored and throw a chain out of the back while the truck was moving. This would cause sparks which, to us kids, was pretty neat. But soon that wasn't good enough, so we would step over the tailgate and hang off the bumper of the back of the truck and step on the chain with one of our shoes so the chain would make even more sparks—*dangerous, right!* I guess now, looking back, since we all took turns (except for Laura), we are all lucky to be alive today. There was no supervision at all. Maybe my mom was too busy or just did not care.

The road took us to 18-wheeler stops, one after the other. You see, I knew my mom had a trade of buffing, polishing, and shining the rims of the big rigs. What I did not know was that she had a side business. As a young boy, I would wonder why when my mom was supposed to be working on the rims of the truck, which were obviously on the outside of the vehicle, she sometimes would be in the cab. Only when I got older did I get to read her file. It stated that my biological mother was a prostitute. When I read that it all made sense. Growing up in this time of my life, I remember not having enough to eat, as mentioned already, sleeping in the back of cars or trucks, as it were, and wearing the same clothes for days and weeks at a time. Reading this, if you have never experienced it, you might think this was pretty bad, but with the exception of being hungry (this was bad), this was what we knew.

Sometimes, when we were lucky, we would stay in hotel rooms for a short span of time. It was at one of these hotel stays that my life made a turn for the worse (or so I thought at the time). From what I remember, a person staying in the next room complained that the kids next door were being too loud. That complaint got the ball rolling on our long stint in foster care. The police showed up and took us to Jefferson County Department of Human Resources in Birmingham, Alabama. I would like to make this statement now— that is, I may not remember all the foster homes I stayed in and the exact order in which I went to stay there, but I will do the best I can. So here we go. I'm pretty sure from the get-go that we stayed in group homes, not foster homes. It's really hard for DHR to find a foster home for multiple children, especially four of them. Group homes are where a bunch of foster kids stay when DHR can't find traditional foster homes. The closest thing I can compare these to are orphanages. The group homes were okay. I mean, it did give us a steady food supply, a place to lay our heads at night and a roof over our heads, but other than that, not much. The attention a little boy like me needed who missed his mommy and did not know why all this was happening to him was just not there. I remember playing bumper pool, going to a community swimming pool, and stopping up the toilet with newspaper because they ran out of toilet paper and blaming it on my older brother (who got in huge trouble). I still feel bad about that today.

CHAPTER 2

Many Different Homes

One of the first traditional foster homes I remember staying in was in Huntsville, Alabama. Somehow, some way—correction—by the providence of God, I was placed under the responsibility of Agape. Agape is a church of Christ–affiliated foster care organization. They have many locations, but the one I fell under was located in Huntsville. So because of this, the first home I really remember is the Browns'. Ray and Pat Brown had three children of their own and one African-American foster baby, whom they later adopted. They attended Memorial Parkway church of Christ, also in Huntsville. This particular church was unlike any others that I have ever seen or heard. The elders saw fit to purchase a house near the church building and use it for foster care ministry. The deal was, if a member of the church would keep foster children, then they could live there rent-free. If I'm not mistaken, I think the Browns took in all four of us in the beginning. Wow, what special people they were and are! What I remember the most about Ms. Pat was that she was a very loving, emotional, and efficient mom. She would cry at the drop of a hat. She is also, definitely, one of the most compassionate people I know. Oh yeah, one other thing about her—she could pinch you with her toes like no one else. *Ouch!* Ray was a great father figure and a great man. Ray and Pat were wonderful parents. They taught us who God was, how He loves us, and how to talk to Him. One more distinct memory I have of this home—it seemed like once a week we would go to this hole-in-the-wall drive-up-only fast-food joint called Beefy's near the house. It had some really good burgers and the best curly fries ever. *Yum!* When we got our food, we would get to sit on the folded-down tailgate of the old station wagon (for the older generation, you know the one—*Brady Bunch*). We ate while Mom drove very slowly home. I still call them Mom and Dad today; I have asked them to give their experience on why they became foster parents, how it was, and their perspective on being my foster parents. This is what they wrote:

Our Life as Foster Parents

We got into foster care in hopes of giving children a chance to grow spiritually, and to face society with two choices: their life as they already knew it and how their parents had already shaped it for them or by allowing the Lord to help them turn their life into something better by making other choices. We wanted to help children have some idea of what a Christian home can be like. We had talked about getting into childcare even before we were married because of the childhood experiences that Pat had in her home life, and the time she and her brothers had spent in a childcare program. We didn't give any thought to the two different backgrounds we came from but were just enthusiastic about the prospects of trying to make a difference in children's lives who were in need of a stable home environment. When we had been married for just a couple of months, we approached Van Ingram, who had been the social worker at the Mt. Dora Christian Home and Bible School where Pat had lived for about a year before meeting Ray, and he told us that we needed to spend more time getting to know each other and giving more thought to what we would be committing to. He was the director of the Tennessee Children's Home at that time, so we waited for about a year, talked and prayed about it during that time, and approached him again after we had been married for a year. He was then agreeable to allowing us to start working as house parents for a group of thirteen little boys from six to twelve years old, at the children's home. We started out with the attitude that we would be able to conquer the world but quickly learned that each child had their own emotional baggage, which we were often unable and ill equipped to handle. We soon realized that social workers and other people with more training and experience than we had were needed to give the kind of help that most of the children were in need of. We voiced these opinions to the board of directors of the children's home, which caused problems regarding how best to care for the children. This disagreement raised other issues which resulted in us having to leave our work at the children's home after almost two years. We were devastated and had a hard time dealing with having to break the bond with the children we had grown to care for so much.

The next phase of our lives led us to spending six years in the air force, during which time Pat's two youngest brothers lived with us as teenagers, and to having three children of our own. After that, we once again contacted Van Ingram, who was then the director of Agape of North Alabama in Huntsville, about getting a reference from him to apply for work as house parents in the childcare program of Madison church of Christ in Madison, Tennessee. Before giving us a reference, he asked that we come to Huntsville and look at the work of Agape and the childcare program at Memorial Parkway church of Christ. When we did that, we decided to move to Huntsville instead and began working with the program there. We moved into a group home to care for up to about six foster children. After working there for about two years, we felt the need to get out of the program because our own children needed some one-on-one attention because they had started feeling neglected by all the time we were needing to devote to the foster children. We had never taken into account how much our own children would have to give up and that they would have to set aside their own needs in order for the needs of the foster children to be taken care of. We finally did realize this only when our own children, who were between five and nine years old at the time, told us they were feeling neglected, and they wanted us to get out of foster care.

We decided as a family unit to get back into foster care after about three years. We were told a family of four would be coming to our home, which was Richard and three of his siblings. They came, as most children did, with the clothes on their back, and a few of their belongings. We remember one instance with Richard when he was outside playing with a friend across the street. Pat called him to come to supper, but he kept on playing and disregarded her call. She called repeatedly with no response from him, and finally she hurriedly went down ten steps, across the driveway and to the neighbor's yard. She picked up Richard, carried him back across the street, put his little feet down beside the entrance to the door, and said, "Obedience is when I call, you come!" That was the last time we had any problem like that. Another memorable occasion occurred with Richard regarding his fear of immunization shots. Because this fear was known, we were able to enlist the help of the nurses at the health clinic where the shots were to be given. After entering the facility through a back door so Richard wouldn't recognize where he was, one of the male nurses was able to "lovingly restrain" him by holding Richard on his lap and crossing his arms and legs over Richards, so the shots could be given without breaking the needle.

After about six months, we were again faced with issues regarding our own children, but this time it was due to personality clashes.

We then made the decision to once again get out of foster care permanently, because we were planning to adopt one of our foster children. Again saying good-bye to Richard and his family would be a sad occasion as it had been with other foster children. We usually were not allowed to make contact with those children again, but Richard and his siblings returned to the childcare program at Memorial Parkway church with a different foster family, and we were able to stay in contact with him as he grew. We were later privileged to be a part of his wedding, and the rest of his story.

Over the years as we have been involved with foster care and the many children Pat has provided day care for, as well as our own children, we have learned they are all unique and different, and each one offers a new challenge. So when people ask for our advice on raising children, our normal response is to say, we knew nothing when we started, and we still know nothing now.

Ray and Pat Brown

Thank you, Mom, Dad, and family, for all that you did for me, my siblings, and foster children in general. We, foster children need more people like you. Also, thank you for what you did for this book. I love you.

After we left the Browns' house, we went to a group home that was on a hill. We only stayed there a short time, so I don't remember what town this was in, but I don't think it was in Huntsville. Keep in mind that as I progress through my foster homes, the years are going by, and I am getting older, so I will remember more about the homes in the reverse order. What I remember about this place are two things: one, this was where I first learned how to tie my shoes, and two; I had a roommate who had some issues. Our room was somewhat like a motel room. It was in the shape of a square with two beds side by side and a small bathroom in front of the foot of our beds. One morning I woke up and smelled something awful. So, just like anyone else would do, I started investigating. What I found was that the kid took a dump on the other side of his bed. This didn't make any sense to me because the bathroom was literally less than ten feet in front of our bed. I let someone know and he got in big trouble.

The next home I stayed in was in Florence, Alabama. The foster mom's name was Darlene, but I can't remember the foster dad's name. I do remember that he was the preacher for a small church of Christ congregation near some railroad tracks beside a highway on the way to Henderson, Tennessee, from Huntsville, Alabama. It was at this house, as a little boy, I started working out and flexing my work ethic. This family would have my foster mom's parents come and visit. During one of these visits, the foster granddad saw me doing a chore I was asked to do and to my surprise, when I was finished, he gave me five dollars. I think, just about every other time that man would come over, I would go outside and start picking up sticks out of the yard. Although I can't remember their names, I know that I made my first really good childhood friends at this home.

The next home I stayed in was one of those I stayed in the longest. Jim and Sharon McLaughlin were the parents' names. The really neat thing about this foster home was they too attended Memorial Parkway church of Christ, and so can you guess what happened. Yep, I got my old room back. How neat was that? Jim and Sharon had two biological children who were married and out of the house. When we moved in it was me, Laura, and my older brother. Neda decided not to move with us because she and our brother were not getting along. At this point in my life, I was a sweet, tenderhearted little boy who did not require too much attention. My brother, however, did. Now, for some more history about my family. I told you already that my first memories were the five kids my mom and my dad had (including Michael). Well, this was actually the second man my mom had kids with. My biological mother had ten kids—five from one man and the other five with my father. As you can imagine, she had some issues. I know for a fact that she had an alcohol problem. I remember her sneaking alcohol into some shelters that we stayed in by putting it in soft-drink cans, not to mention her wetting the bed. The file I told you about earlier stated the same thing. One day while watching TV, Sharon saw a 20/20 show on fetal alcohol syndrome. She immediately thought of our brother. She said almost all the symptoms they named in the show, she saw in him. Although unofficial, she diagnosed my brother with fetal alcohol syndrome. I only tell you this to show you that my brother did, indeed, require a lot of attention and instead of Sharon calling Agape or DHR to request an immediate removal or throwing in the towel; she decided to try and work with him and help him as much as she could. You can see the heart she had. A lot of people might have said, "Yes, I did sign up to be a foster parent, but I did not sign up to deal with something like this, so he has to go." So, what did I do? Monkey see, monkey do. Because I was feeling left out, I started acting out to get attention. I remember one day at dinnertime Sharon prepared spaghetti with meat sauce, and I refused to eat. She did not force me to eat, but she did make me sit in front of my plate at the dinner table until everyone else had finished. Soon after seeing and smelling it, I picked up my fork and started eating. I even asked for seconds. Oh, by the way, you'll never guess what my favorite food of all time is to this day. Yep, it's spaghetti with meat sauce. I really loved this home. Jim and Sharon had major impacts on the rest of my life. I will refer to them now as Mom and Dad. First, Dad was the first man to take me and my brother fishing. It was out of a flat-back canoe with a two-horsepower motor on the back. I am still passionate about fishing today. Next, they planted a seed. I hope you, as my readers, will also plant this same seed with your kids/foster kids. The seed they planted at a very young age has grown over the years into, potentially, my second book, *From the Foster Care Club to the Couple Comma Club (1,000,000): My Journey with God.* I'm not a millionaire yet, but thanks to this seed and if the good Lord sees fit to continue to bless us like He has, my wife and I are well on our way to financial prosperity. I'll let Dad tell you about that seed:

The Daddy Bank

The idea for the daddy bank came when our girls were small. They were getting an allowance, and when they got the allowance, they would spend it at a store as soon as they got it. It did not matter what kind of store. They were required to save some money for church collection, but the rest was spent as quickly as possible on junk or candy.

This is when I offered to give them a part of their allowance and put the rest into a notebook. Each month I would add the interest and ask them how much they wanted to spend. The interest rate was set at 10 percent per month to encourage them to have a substantial gain by saving. Tatia saved some of hers and soon was getting more in interest than she was getting in allowance in any particular month. Lora did not save and soon saw that Tatia had a lot more money than she did. Lora started saving some of her allowance to keep up with her older sister.

The use of the daddy bank allowed them to have access to the money whenever they wanted if they saw something they wanted to buy. Putting the money into a savings account at a bank did not allow for that kind of access. The bank interest rate is too low to provide the kind of incentive that is needed for younger children.

When we did the same thing for our foster children, some took advantage and others could not keep from spending almost as soon as they got the money. Richard was different; he did save most of the allowance money. The amount he saved at 10 percent interest per month became too much, and I had to put a maximum on the amount that would receive interest.

Jim McLaughlin

Now that I am older, I have tweaked this daddy bank some. This is mostly modeled after the ideas of Dave Ramsey and his book *The Total Money Makeover*. First, I would not call it an allowance—Jim called it that—but it really wasn't because if we didn't do our chores, we were not allowed to get our money. I would call it our job or our responsibilities money. Second, Jim always showed us the money and its interest on a little flip notebook. I would show them their responsibility money in actual cash, then hand them their interest in cash, and then store it in an envelope-like system with different categories on each—for example, play money, save money, give money, interest-earned money, etc. Jim did, indeed, plant the seed of compounding interest in my head at a very young age and it has paid dividends. I want to take that idea to the next level with our kids and plant not only the seed of compounding interest, but also budgeting and giving or tithing. Just think about how far ahead of the curve your kids would be financially if their parents used this system too.

The reason I made becoming a millionaire a goal is simple; I thought it would be neat to go from sleeping in the back of cars to becoming a millionaire and then writing a book about it. Who doesn't like a good rags-to-riches story? I know I do! It is that simple. I live in America, and I know we have our problems, but I still truly believe that this is the best country in the world to live in and have this goal become a reality, and I want to take advantage of this! Being wealthy is not bad, evil, or criminal. I understand that some people in this world have money and allow money to rule their hearts and head, but godly people can be wealthy as long as they remember where their wealth comes from—God—and they are just stewards of the blessings He has given them. I do realize that there are wealthy people out there who have good morals, who made their money honestly, and who may not believe in God. We got into the rental business when I was about twenty-one and, as you have read, was taught about compounding interest at a very young age. My wife and I have always had an entrepreneurial spirit, so again, if the Lord sees fit, we will be millionaires. Oh, by the way, even if I don't reach my goal of becoming a millionaire, I will still have a mansion over the hilltop when I die. This happens to be my most important goal in life, which, unlike being wealthy on earth, will last for eternity!

As stated before, my tenure at the Mclaughlin's house lasted longer than any of the previous places I had called home. I got there when I was seven years old and left when I was eleven. This was the home where I met my very best childhood friend. His name was

Wes. It seemed like every weekend we were at each other's house. I remember us talking, like best friends do, about how neat it would be if we were brothers. My time at Mom and Dad's house was really productive. I learned a lot about life and, as you have already heard, a whole lot about finance. I wanted to mention one more thing about these parents, and what they taught me that I treasure more than anything else. Although not perfect, spiritually I knew that they both loved the Lord and made Him the center of our lives. I have asked them to give their perspective of why they became foster parents and what it was like for them to be my foster parents. This is what they wrote:

> Richard, his older brother and two sisters had lived in the children's home owned by the Memorial Parkway church of Christ from December 1988 until the end of May 1989. They were living with the Browns. When the Browns moved out of the home at the end of the school year, the siblings were moved to homes in Florence. Richard's older brother and older sister were placed in the same home and Richard and Laura were placed in the same home. Memorial Parkway church of Christ was looking for new foster parents to move into the home and Jim and I decided we would move in. After we moved into the home, AGAPE asked us to take Richard's older brother back in the home. I wanted to bring the siblings back together, so I requested AGAPE to send them all back. Neda did not want to move back. I was told she didn't want to live with Richard's older brother. Richard and Laura were moved by the end of

December 1989. I suppose no one asked if they wanted to move. Richard didn't say much but didn't appear to be very happy at first. I remember after he had been there a short time, I had to deal with a problem. My mother-in-law was visiting with us when I called everyone to the table, Richard did not come. I went to his room and asked him to come and eat, but he said, "No!" I told him to just come sit at the table and he wouldn't have to eat, so he came to the table and sat down. I put spaghetti on his plate, and we were all talking and ignoring Richard. In a few minutes, he grabbed his fork and started eating like he hadn't eaten all day. After that incident, I never had any trouble getting him to the table. Spaghetti ended up being one of his favorite dishes. My mother-in-law moved to Huntsville the next year. Richard, Laura, and Richard's older brother would spend Friday night with her one at a time. She would always take them out to eat. Richard wanted a buffet all you can eat. She commented on how he liked to eat. Richard was seven years old and in the first grade when he came to live with us. We enrolled him in Madison Academy, a private Christian school, and he thrived. He was well liked by his classmates and he was always the teacher's pet. He always tried to please his teachers. Richard was always self-motived to do well in school. Richard was in Boy Scouts and seemed to enjoy that. A huge part of our life was the spiritual part. We were in church service every time the doors were open unless we were sick. I would have scripture reading and prayer at bedtime. Richard learned a lot about the Bible when he lived with us. He also attended a Christian school where he had Bible every day. He had wonderful Christian women as his teachers. I have always been proud of Richard's good character even when he first came to live with us. Richard lived with us from age seven until he turned eleven. Many trips were made to Booneville, Mississippi, where my relatives live. We always went there on Thanksgiving and Christmas. We would visit my mother other times of the year. Richard was crazy about my two granddaughters, Caitlin and Haley. They loved him, too. Richard also loved cats. We had two cats at one time. He especially loved our cat Rambo. Richard learned how to save money by what my husband called "the daddy bank." We kept foster children for a couple of years when we lived in Memphis, Tennessee. At that point, our girls were very young. Our two girls were grown and married when we moved into the children's home in Huntsville, Alabama. We tried to raise our foster children like we raised our girls. We tried to treat them like we would treat our own. We lived our life like the children were our biological ones. Richard and Laura were the only foster children that lived with us for four and a half years. For different reasons, we had kids that came and went. Sometimes, that is just how foster care is. I suppose Richard had lived with us for so long that he never thought about leaving the home. He must have been devastated when we told them that we were moving to Utah. Jim had been having financial difficulties with his company. Because of these problems, he ended up having to sell his company, and he signed a contract agreeing to work with the company that bought it for three years. This company was particularly interested in my husband's shoe-covering machine. They decided to move the shoe covering machine to North Salt Lake, Utah, and Jim had to go with it. Jim moved to Utah in January of 1994, and I stayed in the home until Richard and Laura finished the school year. We had to tell the children we were moving out of the church's home because Jim had to move so soon. Richard did not take the news very well, but I could understand why. All those years living with us had been very easy, but dealing with Richard the last few months became very difficult. I handled it the best I could and certainly could understand why he acted the way he did. Richard wrote a sweet letter apologizing for his behavior after I moved to Utah. When we were visiting our children and grandchildren in Huntsville, Alabama, later in the year of 1994, we ran across the Odens at a restaurant. They expressed interest in adopting Richard. I believe it was the providence of God that he and Laura were adopted by the Odens. I truly believe because of the providence of God that all things have worked out for Richard.

Sharon McLaughlin

Thank you, Mom, Dad, and family, for all that you did for me, my siblings, and foster children in general. Also, thank you so much for planting that seed you did. I'm sure my kids one day will thank you for that as well, but most importantly, thank you for showing me how to live a life that has God at the center of it. We foster children need more people like you. Lastly, thank you for what you did for this book. I love you.

As Mom said, Mom and Dad had to stop being foster parents because of Dad's job. When we lived there, he owned his own business. He invented a machine that made shoe covers for hospitals. A company bought that machine two or so years prior to them moving. That company agreed not to move the machine or relocate my dad for those two years. Well, those two years were up when I turned eleven. They moved the machine and him to Utah. I was devastated, and I turned from a sweet, tenderhearted boy into a heathen child. I guess, at that age, being that I was with them for four-and-a-half years, longer than anyplace else. I thought and hoped I would be there forever. In foster care, as a child, after you get over the shock of being taken away from your biological parents, moving around a lot, and getting your heart broken multiple times, you start adjusting to the situation, and you get comfortable and let your guard down. All I wanted was somewhere to call home. I wanted to be in one place, not having to worry about moving. I wanted so badly to have stability and permanency. I really thought I had all that at this home. I didn't understand why mom and dad would do this to me. I couldn't, or more likely, wouldn't, at this age, face the fact that this wasn't their fault. At this point in my life, all I knew was moving: moving with my biological mom—knock, knock, knock—and the police were at the front door with a social worker from DHR to say, "Pack your things (usually in a single black garbage bag), you're moving to group homes, then to foster homes." After a while, I felt like it wasn't worth my time or effort to make new friends or to get attached to new parents just to get my heart broken. *I was very angry!* I began lashing out with some very hurtful words and actions.

My anger got the best of me when I was in foster care. Unfortunately, for my sister Laura, I would usually take it out on her. I remember her saying something I did not like on the way to school one day so I smacked her across the face and busted her nose. I didn't mean to bust her nose, but I did mean to smack her. This incident caused my first of many sessions with a counselor. From the get-go as a foster child, I hated the idea of talking to someone about my problems. They were mine and I could deal with them. My solution was to bottle them all up inside me and never let them out. The problem with that was they did come out. Whether I wanted to admit it or not they came out in my lashing out with my words and my actions. Let me say this to every foster kid reading this book: I get it. I was that kid. I have been in your shoes, but take it from me—give these people a chance. Be honest with them. If you don't know why you are angry, tell them, but if you do know why, tell them the truth. Don't say, "I don't know." It's a cop-out. Let them help. From my own experience, I know they helped me. This particular counselor is a man I love and respect to this day. His name is Lonnie Jones. He was also my youth minister at Memorial Parkway church of Christ. One of the things he taught me I will never forget. I told him Laura made me smack her by saying something I didn't like. He told me that Laura was more powerful than me because she could control what I did by her words if she, indeed, make me smack her. Being her stronger big brother, I did not like the thought of that. He taught me that a powerful person had the power to control his own behavior and not let anybody else have that power. Lonnie is now a licensed professional counselor and I have asked him to say a few words about me. This is what he wrote:

It's one of those strange things. You see a student, and you just know they are different. Often "different" doesn't always mean good. But in Richard's case, it was. I remember meeting with him to discuss some "conflicts" with foster parents. But even as a young boy, Richard was able to take unreasonable expectations and weather the storm.

If I could describe Richard with a Bible verse, it would be the context of Philippians 4:13. This verse is often used in athletics, but in context, it is the epitome of Richard's attitude... or he is the epitome of the verse. No matter what circumstance, no matter what home, no matter what he had, or didn't have this young man seemed content.

As I watched him mature, he weathered being surrounded by lots of instability and drama with a determination to work his way to where he wanted to be. In those days, we had fewer conversations, but then he didn't need them. He was demonstrating a work ethic, a discipline of character and integrity that won the heart of Brittany and the respect of her parents. There is no way to say this and not have it sound a bit awkward, but Greg always struck me as pretty rigid. A rocket scientist (engineer) who saw things as black and white. Ideal or unacceptable. I wasn't sure how Greg would respond to Richard when it came to Brittany. Greg and I were and are friends. He's never given me anything but support. He was and is a guy I can call on for anything. He and I had come from very different worlds. He had sat up late with me at camps. He bought drill bits for me to use in building a climbing wall and cut the first trials to the ropes course on Keel Mountain. During these times, he had learned my story. I came from a poor beginning (that's just money wise; my childhood was exceptional with very good parents). But several people invested in me, gave me a chance... and well, I like to think that Greg saw in Richard what many folks saw in me. In fact I've often thought that Greg wanted to do for Richard what so many had done for me. Greg once told me that he respected me for where I'd come from. I did not grow up privileged. My senior ring is a radiator in a '68 Impala. I made choices to work instead of play ball. I looked under coke machines to get change to eat out when I was in college. I think he saw that that kind of work and determination was the foundation of character. He saw it in Richard... not because he wanted it to be there but because it was undeniably there. He gave him a chance and thus confidence and thus trust and treated him like a man and not a kid. And Richard did not and has not disappointed.

I sit here today and think of Richard and Brittany and don't think of a life we helped change but think of a young man who has changed the life of most of the people he has ever encountered. If I am a small part of influencing that is fine and well, but I really like to think of it in terms of being blessed by knowing him and watching him grow and become the man he is.

Two of my favorite quotes:

These both apply to Richard.

"Experience is not what happens to you but what you do with what happens to you."[2]

"I will do the things that you will not in order to continue to do the things that you cannot."[3]

Lonnie Jones

Thank you, Lonnie, for everything you have done. You have had a huge impact on my life and so many others. God has used you to make this world a better place. One of my many goals is to make my small mark in the world and do the same thing. You have definitely been an excellent ambassador for God's kingdom. As we military would say, "Carry on, sir!"

My life up to this point was typical for kids who entered foster care, and TPR (termination of parental rights) had occurred. A lot of moving around and even more of not understanding what was taking place in my life. I had many questions. What was TPR? Why wasn't I with my mom? What did she do, or not do, for us not to be with her? Was this my fault? When a kid like me has no answers, then he starts making some up in his head. I don't remember anybody sitting us down and explaining why we were in foster care. I think this was due to them thinking we were too young to understand or because it was a very uncomfortable situation to discuss, and/or they did not

---

[2]   Aldous Huxley; English novelist; 1894-1963

[3]   Author unknown

30

know how. Now that I have typed this last sentence and read it back, I think the correct answer would be all of the above. *This was a big mistake!* As a child in foster care, I just wanted someone to help me understand what in the world was going on. Even if they did a bad job, it would have helped to know the foster parents tried. I would encourage all foster parents if you can answer some of the questions a foster child has, do it. They probably have some, if not all, of the same questions I did. Sit them down and have a talk. Do the best you can and be honest. Reassure them that no matter what they have heard, this wasn't their fault, and don't sugarcoat it. The situation, in the kids' eyes, obviously is not good. Tell them the real deal—the truth.

After we left the McLaughlins', we moved to Gardendale, a city outside of Birmingham, Alabama. My foster parents there were Ray and Jackie Samples. Although I did not spend much time there, it was an absolutely wonderful home. What I remember the most about this home—my tush remembers it too—was that one day I was being very disrespectful to Ray. I looked him in the eye and said, "You won't touch me or I'll tell DHR on you," and before I could get the letter *R* in DHR out, he gave me what I needed—two times. We never had a problem again. As a matter of fact, had it not been for my little sister Laura, I think they would have adopted me. Oh, I want to mention something now that you probably already figured out. Remember when I told you it was hard for DHR to find a home that would take four kids? Well, after we left the McLaughlins' our luck ran out, so they had to split us up. Typically, they will send the older siblings together and the younger siblings together, and that's exactly what they did to us. A few things about this home I loved were, first, weekends at Smith Lake in Cullman, Alabama. The Samples had a trailer on the lake with a private dock and a boat. I found a three-foot-by-three-foot or so piece of Styrofoam, which was about a foot and a half thick. I would sit on the front of it with my fishing pole and get my sister or buddy to sit on the back and kick her feet. This was my first fishing boat. It was awesome! Second, this was the first home I got to play organized football, which I later played all four years in high school. Next, I remember not being happy about the church situation. Ray and Jackie were Methodists, and as you already know, my background was church of Christ. I was very upset I had to go to their church, and do you know what they did? They made arrangements for me to go to a local church of Christ while they attended their church. This worked out or would have worked out really well, but Laura and I moved before the ball on that got rolling. But, the fact that they were going to do that meant a whole lot to me. Finally, right before I left, I asked them to let me have a spot in their yard so I could grow a garden, and they agreed. I took a little hand pick with a broken handle (the broken handle required me to get on my hands and knees) and I plowed it, and got it planted, but then we moved. Years later, I randomly went to visit them. Guess where the vegetables they had in the fridge came from? Yep, my garden. That was pretty neat to see that they took my idea and ran with it. I asked them to write about their foster-parent experience and a little about me. This is what they wrote:

> My name is Jackie Samples. My husband Ray and I felt a nudge to become foster parents in 1989. After praying and discussing it, we had a family meeting with our three daughters, twelve, thirteen, and fifteen at the time to get their input. They all agreed and seemed excited. We worked through Children's Aid Society (CAS), which is part of United Way. In the course of ten years, we had forty-two children to come through our home, each with their own circumstances and story. Some stayed for

a year or longer; some stayed for only a couple of weeks/months. Children who came through CAS were usually less traumatized. The CAS case workers work with the parent(s) and the children are usually placed in foster care with approval of the parent(s) while the parent works through drug treatment or any other hindrances that prevent them from being responsible, nurturing parents. We were licensed and received our first child in 1990. CAS would periodically be called by Department of Human Services (DHS) to "borrow" foster homes as DHS foster homes would be filled to the limit at the time. Many of our children were from DHS. Our first child was an infant directly from the hospital from birth. One of our children was brought to us at night, around 8:30 by a policeman. The child was on the streets of Birmingham with no place of residence. The police called DHS, and they had no place available, so they called CAS, and then we were called. In some cases, it was very disheartening to have the children be returned to previous home. In other cases, it was comforting to learn the parent had overcome their problem and could now take care of their child in a loving manner. In the difficult times of children returning to questionable home situations, we just had to pray for them to be safe and loved and accept that we were just the "stepping stone" they needed at that time. I still think of them all and pray they are in a good home situation.

I felt a kindred spirit with our foster children. When I was a child, I was tossed from my mother to my grandmother, preferring to stay with my grandmother. I lived with her most of my life, until I was about eight years old. Then my mother took me and would not let me go back. My home life after that was very dysfunctional, actually abusive in some respect. As a foster parent, I learned to admire the stubborn children because I knew they would survive their circumstances better than the more sensitive children. I learned to appreciate that I was called stubborn as a child, because I now know I would not have survived well had I not been stubborn.

A particular situation we were asked to take two siblings—Richard, twelve, and his sister Laura, ten, at the time. They came to us from a foster home they had been in for five years, so this was a very tough move for them. Just try to imagine going to a strange home, strange people, strange/different ways to live, and you really have no say in the matter. Everything you own is in a plastic garbage bag. You don't know whether the home you are going to is as good, better or worse. I still have to fight the urge to cry when I think of all these children. I know exactly how they feel. And it isn't fair! But, back to Richard and Laura. They really were pleasant children, didn't seem to have any hang-ups. Laura collected thimbles and was taught how to sew by her previous foster mom. They really seemed to have a close relationship, and I feel it was very painful for them both to be separated. I sew but it just wasn't the same for Laura. Richard loved the outdoors and sports. We had a place on Smith Lake that we all enjoyed going to on the weekends. Richard would float up and down the lake on a piece of Styrofoam like Huckleberry Finn! We occasionally kept a young boy whose mother was single and struggling. He and Richard had a good time together. My husband, Ray, built a tree house in one of our big pecan trees that they really enjoyed playing in. And Ray signed them both up for summer football together.

There seemed to be something uncomfortable for Richard in a previous possible foster/adoption situation, but he never spoke of it. I remember a trip home from taking Richard and Laura to a counseling session. We were having a conversation, and I asked how the counseling went, and they both said they didn't talk to the counselor. They just sat in the office and wouldn't answer questions. When I asked, "Why not?" they said, "What do you care." That broke my heart. Fighting tears, I told them I did care! We seemed to be closer after that incident. They needed to know I cared, and I wanted them to know that I cared. They didn't know how well I understood their situation.

Richard and Laura stayed with us through the summer of that year, waiting for a foster home to become available in their former school district. There were a few obstacles with them staying with us. We were from different church backgrounds, and they didn't seem to like going to our church, and we didn't have separate bedrooms they could stay in for long term residence. I would love for them both to have stayed with us indefinitely if situations had been more favorable.

I feel God called us to be part of all these children's lives, for some reason, for that period of time. Maybe we will know His purpose one day. But for now, all these children will always have a special place in our hearts, and it was a blessing to be part of their lives for the time we had them. I learned more from each of them than they learned from me, I am sure. I pray for them all and wonder at times how they are doing in life. I pray they found a safe, happy, loving home. I am very proud of how Richard and Laura have succeeded in their lives so far, and will continue to pray for their futures.

I urge all who have ever thought about becoming foster parents to just do it. You will be blessed in more ways than you can ever imagine! None of us are perfect, nor do we always know what to do in any particular situation, but do the best you can and let them know you love them and leave the rest in God's hands.

Ray and Jackie Samples

Thank you Ray, Jackie, and family for your ministry in foster care. We foster kids who need good homes and would definitely benefit from more good foster homes like yours!

From Gardendale we moved to West Limestone in Limestone County, Alabama. Ann Bobo was her name. She was an experienced, sweet little lady who happened to be widowed, and I had a problem with that. I guess, up to this point in my foster care tenure, I had been spoiled. What I mean by this is the fact that all the rest of my foster homes had a mom and a dad. You know the old saying, "You don't know what you have until you don't have it anymore." Well, this was one of those times. I knew it wasn't her fault. However, I also knew I needed a positive father figure in my life, but they didn't ask me. Ms. Bobo's home was a good home as well. She had a few foster kids come and go while we stayed there. I remember there being three teenage girls in this home who were sexually active. One came to the home pregnant. Later I was told people were watching her with me because she was always saying she wanted a little brother and she was very touchy-feely and "huggy" with me. They had their guard up. Another girl got into a lot of trouble where sex was involved and I would overhear the other one openly discussing her sex life. I only put this in the book as a warning to all potential or current foster parents. I don't know the actual statistics, but from my personal experience, I do know that sex and experimenting go on in foster care more than your average home, and not just teenagers. There are many reasons. For example, you remember what I did when I saw my older brother acting up, and I would feel left out: monkey see, monkey do. Some of these kids lived a life a lot worse than mine. You may not be able to fathom what they have seen and heard, or what has been done to them. Another reason my wife is quick to point out is, you have a bunch of kids who are not related living under the same roof. To protect the home and the identity of the people involved, I won't mention any names, but before I was a teenager, two new foster kids came to live with us. They were an older brother and a younger sister. The brother was older than me. One day he came to me with his sister and told us that he wanted me and her to do it, and he wanted to watch and that he would tell us what to do. This happens in foster care. It is very real. Have your guard up, be vigilant, and do your very best to eliminate a possible compromised situation.

I still have contact with Mama Ann today. I asked her too if she would give her perspective of being a foster parent, some of the struggles, and what she remembered about me, but we did this a little differently. I interviewed her over the phone. This is what she said:

> I had always thought about fostering children but never got around to it until one day while I was watching TV with one of my daughters. Although I thought she was asleep, but she wasn't. The show was about kids getting murdered by their parents. When it was over, Misty, my daughter, asked if after those kids got to heaven, could they come live with us? I had to explain to her how all that worked, but that very moment, I decided that fostering was what we were going to do. I got my first foster care license with DHR in Decatur, Alabama. I wanted to teach these children discipline and morals. I had a reputation in the foster care community that I would take any kid, so some were really bad, with a lot of baggage. They lived rough lives. Some were in gangs and a lot were physically and sexually abused. Over my foster care tenure, we fostered over sixty kids. During that time the rule was if you fostered

kids you could not adopt them. Back then we thought that rule stank, so we organized foster families and tried to get that rule changed. I'm not sure how much direct effect that we had, but that rule did get changed soon after our actions! I always had the maternal feelings toward my foster children, but I also knew my place, and that was to be temporary parents. When my kids would leave my home, our family would often cry buckets of tears, but I knew I had to let them go. Looking back on it now, it was definitely worth it!

When Richard and his sister, Laura, came to live with us, they were different. I was surprised to hear they lived in so many different homes. If I had to guess after they lived in my home for a little while, I would have said they only lived in one or two foster homes. They just didn't have the baggage some of my other children did. Their appearance and behavior impressed me the most! I am really proud of the way Richard has turned out, and it warms my heart that he is paying this forward!

Ann Bobo

Thank you, Mama Ann, for your ministry in foster care. You truly made an impact on my life and many others! God bless!

While I was at Mama Ann's home, I started feeling really bad about the way I treated Mom McLaughlin. I told Mama Ann about how I treated her and how bad I was feeling about it. She encouraged me to write a letter and mail it to her, and that's exactly what I did. As mentioned before, I am thirty-one now while writing this book. I asked Mom McLaughlin if she still had the letter I wrote to her about 20 or so years before, and she said she did. I will put it in word-for-word; remember, I was twelve or so when I wrote it:

9-27-1994
Dear Mom
How are you doing? I am OK. Is it neat up thiere in Utah., is it better than Alabama. I wanted to say thank you for every thing you did for me. You know all Im talking about.
Gess what we got, a kitten it is black and white his name is Angel. He is nice and he pears a lot. I lie him but not as much as I do Rambo. We also have a dog his name is Zeak his is mean I don't like him.
Laura talks about you a lot and I do to. You are the best mom out of all the moms were before you and after we left you. You know when I said some bad stuff to you at the time I was saying them. I thought I ment them but know that I left I know I didn't Im sorry for all the bad stuff I said to you. Laura said to tell you he and she missis you. Your son forever Richard
PS Please wright back.

Wow, reading that back brings up some very emotional memories. I was very angry, as already stated, when they moved to Utah. If I am honest with myself, at that age, I really thought that me being so ugly was the reason they went through with that move. I meant every word of this letter, but in the back of my mind while writing it, this was a last-ditch effort for them to accept my apology and come back and get Laura and me and keep us forever. This, of course, did not happen. What did happen was the plan God had for me for the rest of my life. So keep reading, and you will see that plan. Also reading that back makes me incredibly thankful for spell-check and a great editor!

During our stay at Ms. Bobo's house, I became good friends with my social worker's son. He happened to be about my age. Skip, my social worker at the time, went out of her way to help us get to spend some time together. To all social workers, I know you can't save them all or help them all. I know from experience, being that I have a rare point of view, that I have experience with social workers as a foster kid and foster parent. I know you are underpaid and overworked, but please go the extra mile where you can. Follow Skip's example; you would be doing even greater work, and your work will become more fulfilling. Most importantly, you would be helping your kids. Be willing to do the same for your foster parent as well.

After we were at Ms. Bobo's house for a while, something strange started happening. It was strange, but really good. Do you remember my best friend Wes from church? He and his family started coming to visit Laura and me from Huntsville, about an hour's drive away. It was awesome to see my best friend, but I had no idea why they started coming to visit, except so Wes and I could continue being best friends. These soon led up to weekend visits at his house for Laura and me. I'll let Wes's mom, Ms. Debbie, tell you what she and her husband, Gerry, had in mind:

Our First Memories of Richard

We first met Richard when he was about six years old. He and his siblings attended church with their foster family. Richard became fast friends with our second son, Wes. He would visit often as their friendship deepened, and the two became best friends. Richard was an active little fellow, and he especially enjoyed playing outdoors. He was happy whenever he was over and laughed easily with our four children. Richard was always respectful and obedient and made the most of every minute. We came to love this little boy through his visits to our home and his interaction with our family. Our hearts were saddened when we learned that Richard and his little sister, Laura, would be leaving the Huntsville area. At this point, Gerry and I never considered becoming foster/adoptive parents.

CHAPTER 3

Decision Point

The Decision to Adopt

It was a night we will never forget! Richard and Laura moved to a new foster home just north of Birmingham. Our family was sad about them leaving the area, especially Wes. Wes began to receive letters from Richard a few weeks later. We remember the excitement that we all felt when Richard's first letter came in the mail. We all read it and cried! It was at this point God began to place the idea of adoption on mine and Gerry's hearts.

A few months passed, and Wes received more letters from Richard. We were filled with mixed emotions each time we read one of the letters. Richard and Laura were not happy, and that tugged at our hearts. We spoke to different people at church about how they were doing during this time, and we learned that they moved once again. This move placed them in a home in western Limestone County.

Wes received a particular touching letter from Richard in the mail. As always, Wes shared the letter with us. Gerry and I read it together, and it brought us both to tears. We then put all our children to bed with our normal nightly routine. Next, we retreated to our bedroom, but neither of us spoke for several minutes. I know that each of us was deep in thought considering the idea of adopting both Richard and Laura. Gerry finally quietly spoke what was on both our hearts: "Do you think we could adopt Richard and Laura?"

This one question would unleash a lengthy discussion between the two of us that lasted well into the early morning hours. We had both privately considered the idea of adoption, and we had both been privately praying about it for several weeks. But, we had been too afraid to open up the discussion. After all, we had four healthy children whom we adored. We weren't licensed for foster care or adoption. We weren't sure we had enough room for two more children. We weren't sure if we could afford to adopt and we didn't know where to begin.

Gerry and I laid in bed that night for hours and talked, cried, and prayed together. We decided that very evening to adopt Richard and Laura. We believe that God had placed this on our hearts and that it was his divine plan. We now knew what we wanted and needed to do. Even though we felt excited and scared and happy and uncertain, it was a relief to reach the decision that had been in our hearts and on our minds during the months since Richard and Laura had left. We were finally able to sleep.

Debbie Oden

Deb,

You've captured it. I read this and remembered the night, even though I haven't revisited it in a long time. I know that in the time between their move to Birmingham and that night, I was so disappointed in so many people, feeling that the church had really let these two kids down. I felt this way for weeks, perhaps months, more so with every letter we received. Eventually, I realized that we too, were part of the church and then I was disappointed in myself. While this wasn't the decision to adopt (that is too big a decision to be entered into rashly or due to guilt), I felt convicted in my own mind.

Later, when we were going through our training as foster/adoptive parents, a well-meaning individual counseled against our going through with the adoption. I think the memory of that original realization that we were part of the church and equally expected to care for fatherless children became a conviction that this was something we had been called to do.

Gerry Oden

So mine and my best friend's conversation became true and we became brothers. Some of you say, "Wow, that's way cool," and others say, "Uh-oh, be careful what you wish for." More importantly, my parents gave me and my sister the permanency that I so desperately wanted and needed. Mom and Dad, thank you so much for doing what you did for me and my sister. You had four children of your own—one happy family. So many other families would have been content with that, but thanks to your loving and compassionate hearts, you guys together gave two children the best gift anyone could give—*a loving, God-fearing, permanent home!* I'm sorry I had my difficulties growing up, but know, the older I get, the more I see and appreciate the sacrifices that you made for us. Mom and Dad, thank you for everything you did for us in our lives, and thank you for what you did for me and my readers in this book. *I love you* and hope, one day, to follow in your footsteps. *I love you, again!*

On May 15, 1995, my name officially changed from Richard Sundown Robert Paul Golec to Richard Paul Oden. I was 12. So now, of course, I lived with the Odens. The adjustment went very well. I had never before experienced what having extended family felt like. It was great. I got two sets of grandparents and a multitude of aunts, uncles, and cousins overnight. They all made me feel like I was born into the family, just like I was another Oden. Thank you all for that, and *Roll Tide!* I have asked my grandparents on my dad's side to write a few words, and this is what they wrote:

> When we first met Richard and his younger sister, Laura, we were all at a birthday party for our granddaughter Jessica. Little did we know Richard and Laura would become our grandchildren too! Our son and daughter-in-law eventually adopted Richard and Laura. They became a much loved and important part of our family. Richard quickly bonded with his new found grandparents, aunts, uncles, and cousins. Over the years, there have been many happy occasions: holidays, birthdays, weddings.

One highlight for us was the year we took Richard and his cousin Kyle on vacation to visit our younger son and his family in Pennsylvania. Richard and Kyle got along famously—getting into mischief and playing with their little cousins.

Early on, it was obvious that whatever Richard did, he worked on it with all his heart and might—whether it was school, football, work, or play. Amazed, and very proud, we watched him graduate college in three years while working three and four jobs. When he set his heart on Brittany, we knew she would become a member of our family, too. He couldn't have chosen better. To see the caring, dedicated young boy become a caring, dedicated husband and father has been one of our greatest joys and many treasured memories.

Mema and Pepa Oden

Thank you all for all your support over the years. I love you all! I really am glad I am part of the Oden clan.

CHAPTER 4

A Permanent Family

My adoptive parents still attended Memorial Parkway Church of Christ, where their son, my brother now, became friends with me. I didn't get my old room back this time, but I did get to reunite with all the people who, on and off, watched me grow up, and that was pretty cool. One man in particular, Greg Parker, who used to be my fifth-grade Bible class teacher, is one of many whom I love and respect to this day.

Growing up officially as an Oden was great. It also did have its trials and tribulations. You know, there was the usual teenage stuff, but for some reason, my mom and I butted heads more than anyone else. Later, while taking classes to get my foster care license, I finally figured out why this might have taken place. The class stated that some kids had a hard time bonding or were butting heads with their parents because the nurturing from the parents was not there as a young child. After hearing that on top of the whole teenage thing and my other issues (mainly, accepting and dealing with my past), it was no wonder we butted heads so much. I love you, Mom and thank you for loving me unconditionally. I really needed that!

CHAPTER 5

Facing Philistines

I was in high school when I got my first job at Winn-Dixie. I knew I was a hard worker and I wanted so badly to show people what I could do. It was a great experience for me. I worked in just about every department a teenager could. I started as a bagger; then stocked frozen food, then dairy, deli, and produce, was a stocker at night and even worked in the pharmacy as a pharmacy tech. But, because I have been blessed with a gregarious personality, my favorite position was where it all started—bagging groceries. I started this job my junior year in high school. While in high school, I also played football and baseball, wrestled, and took taekwondo a couple of nights a week. I made the National Honor Society one year, but for the most part, my grades were average. But considering all I had going on, I was okay with that. I guess one might say I was pretty busy—yet another providence of God! I know God knew I would have a lot on my plate when I got older so he started preparing me for that when I was in high school. Out of everything I did in high school, football taught me the most of life-lessons. I played—or was on the team, I should say—all four years of high school, but I didn't start until my senior year. All good things come to those who wait! I was five foot, eight inches tall and one hundred and thirty pounds sopping wet. Obviously, I was not one of the biggest on the field and I was pretty scared at times, but I got over it and did my job. I was backup quarterback and I started at free safety. To this day I say the coaches put me at free safety not because I was a headhunter, but because they knew I needed the fifteen- to twenty-yard head start. "Face your Philistines"—your fears—deal with them and move on. I definitely was not the biggest, fastest, or most athletic on the field, but the one thing I did have, which made up a lot of ground where I was lacking, was a huge heart. After I finally faced my fears and moved on, I did not care how big you were or how much it might have hurt; I would hit you and do everything in my power to get you on the ground. Sometimes—actually, a lot of times—I would look at a teammate of mine who was about six feet, six inches and around three hundred pounds but was lazy and say to myself, "If I had his frame and my heart, then I would be playing in the NFL on Sundays after my junior year playing college football for The University of Alabama," but I didn't have his frame, all I had was what God had given me. I had my size, my heart, my life, my circumstances, my foster care stint, my moving around a lot, my vulnerable heart, and most importantly, I had my God! In the Scriptures, it reads that God will never give us more than we can bear, "No temptation has overtaken you except such as is common to man; but God is faithful, who will not allow you to be tempted beyond what you are able, but with temptation will also make the way of escape, that you may be able to bear it." (1 Corinthians 10:13). It also states that God will give us everything we need, "Look at the birds of the air, for they neither sow nor reap nor gather into barns; yet your heavenly Father feeds them. Are you not of more value then they?" (Matthew 6:26). So, don't concentrate on what you don't have but focus on what God has blessed you with and do the very best you can with that, and that is exactly what I did! Also, everyone who has played organized football knows the old saying, "When you get knocked down you get right back to your feet and try again." Well, I know it's cliché, but when life knocked me down, I did, indeed, get right back up. But before that, I would pray. I would not throw in the towel. After I was on my feet, I would evaluate the situation and my mistakes and learn from them. When I did that, I knew whatever I did, as long as I learned from it, was not a wasted mistake. On this very point, I also have a shirt on my website www.myfulllifecirclesquared.com that states, "YOU STRESS, YOU FRAY, I STRESS, I PRAY… PRAY WITHOUT CEASING. I THESSALONIANS 5:17"

Lastly, high school football tested my mental and physical limits, which helped me tremendously when I got to Lackland Air Force Base, in San Antonio, Texas, for basic training. Out of about fifty-two trainees, I was the oldest one in my flight at age twenty-eight. I had the highest physical training score, a 98, one sit-up away from a perfect 100. I hate sit-ups, by the way, and I graduated as an honor graduate.

CHAPTER 6

My Sweet Wife, Brittany

The first and second time I came and went and came back to Memorial Parkway church of Christ, I didn't even know she existed. I guess I was too young to care. The third time, however, when I was adopted, I did know she existed and I was old enough to care. We started going out around middle school. I have no idea why they call it this. We were both too young to drive. I think she was twelve and in the seventh grade. I was fourteen and in the eighth grade. She was and is the most beautiful person inside and out.

Brittany and I dated so long that whenever you saw one of us at a church function you saw the other. We were joined at the hip. I was her first and only kiss. I like to ask her a lot who was her best kiss, because I already know the answer. She is also quick to remind me that I was her worst kiss as well.

When Brittany graduated high school and it was time for college she and her dad always had a dream of her going to Freed-Hardeman University in Henderson, Tennessee. This was a church of Christ affiliated university that our congregation would go to for camp during the summers. I always knew that was their plan but when the time came, I, for obvious reasons, did not like it. It was a three-hour drive one-way from Huntsville, where I was going to college, to Freed. There was always that thought in the back of my mind that she would forget about me when she got there and some other guy would be there to fill that void. So, my solution to that problem was to get engaged before she left. I bought the engagement ring about a month before her 18th birthday. The day I bought it her grandparents were in the same store and they saw me. What were the chances of that? You talk about *awkward*! So, I wrapped the ring up and gave it to her as her birthday present. When she opened it and everyone saw that it was a ring, her dad said, "If that is what I think it is, give it back to him" and without hesitation Brittany did. My ongoing joke for years was her dad should have been very happy that I was trying to marry his oldest daughter because if it were his younger one, that event might not have gone so smoothly. I knew Brittany's heart, and she loved her parents, therefore, she obeyed but I felt like it was at my expense. I was angry at him for separating us. I was angry because of my past. Moving around a lot and getting attached to people is something that reflects hard on one's life. Only this time she was moving, not me and that was something he might not have thought of. At the same time, he had to do what he thought was best for his daughter. He later told us that part of him sending her away was a test to see if we were truly committed to each other because we both basically, only dated each other our entire lives. So, she went to Freed, and I stayed in Huntsville. I drove to Freed on occasion. During these drives the trip took me past a church of Christ by some railroad tracks that I thought looked very familiar from somewhere in my past. Eventually, Brittany and I made it to a Sunday morning service at this church where we confirmed that this was, indeed, the church where my foster dad from Florence, Alabama had preached. It took several years for me to let go and stop being angry at Brittany's father for sending her away. Yes, it was her father's decision, but it was his heavenly Father's will. You see, it was hard having a long-distance relationship. However, we did pass that test and it only made our relationship grow that much stronger. Most importantly, once again, God knew we would need this for our future and he used this to prepare us for it. Thank you, Lord.

Sometimes we don't understand why things happen in our lives, but if we are patient, we will see that trials and tribulations are used to prepare us for what is to come down the road.

We dated for seven years and on May 22, 2004, she changed her name from Brittany Jo Parker (yes, the daughter of my fifth-grade Bible class teacher) to Brittany Parker Oden. At our wedding there were several special things that happened. First, about four hundred fifty to five hundred people showed up for it and when they made the announcement, they gave us a standing ovation. Also, when we had the parents seated, we had all these parents seated, too—the Browns, McLaughlins, and Samples and last but not least, my adoptive parents, the Odens. That was something to see! You see, unlike a normal kid, all these parents helped raise me. Brittany and I felt like we needed and wanted to honor them at our wedding. Without each and every one of them taking me in and teaching me, who knows what would have become of me. It takes very special people to do what they did—all of them—and for that, we felt like it was the least we could do.

I knew from early on I wanted and was going to marry her. My parents and sibling will attest that I would go around the house announcing that I would. I guess it's my personality. When I have my mind set on something, I am too stubborn not to do it. In just about every big decision I make, I put it on the "Richard's return on investment" scale. Over our dating years, I had paid thousands of dollars in gas, food, jewelry, and opportunity cost (time). All that was on my mind was an investment and my return on investment was for her to be my wife. So, if she said no, someone was going to die. Luckily, no one had to because she was very excited and pleased that I had asked her. Of course, she said yes. By the way, I got the better half of this marriage deal! Speaking of when I asked her to marry me, it was Easter of 2003. I had nine plastic eggs with something inside each one. The tenth egg was a crystal egg with the engagement ring inside, and of course, because I'm me and to try to be funny, I had a bonus plastic egg as the eleventh one. The first one she opened had a payday inside it with a note that said, "For all the paychecks I will be handing over to you." The second one had a Snickers bar in it, and the note said, "For all the laughs we have shared and are going to share together." The third had a Baby Ruth and it read, "Because one day, you will have my baby." The fourth had a fishing lure, and the note said, "Because you're a keeper." The fifth had Sweet Tarts candy in the shape of hearts, and it said, "Because you're my sweetheart." The tenth crystal egg had, of course, the engagement ring. Wow! I did well remembering six out of ten eggs. I really don't remember what I put in the other four. Typical man, right, ladies? Sorry, it was, or will be, eleven plus years ago. I did do the whole "get down on one knee" thing. The bonus egg had a note on the outside and the inside. The outside note said, "To be opened only if you said yes to egg number ten." The inside note said, "To be used after we are married," and you can guess what was in it. On a serious note, I knew one day Brittany would make an excellent wife and mother. She was and is my best friend with a great, loving heart. Most importantly, I knew that she was the one who would help me get to heaven, and I, in return, would help her do the same. In the Bible, it says, "Who can find a virtuous wife? For her worth is far above rubies. The heart of her husband safely trusts her; so he will have no lack of gain." (Prov. 31:10–11) I tell her and the people around her that, for me, she is that wife and so much more. I love you, honey, thank you so much for spending the rest of your life with me and my baggage, letting me serve my country, and coming with me on my full life circle, squared. I have asked her to say a few words and this is what she wrote:

> Richard has been asking me to write my part for his book for years now. I am finally writing this the night before he is to turn his

book over to the publisher. I, also, have not read his book in its entirety. He has read me portions, but I have not read the whole thing. At the present time, we have just recently taken a new foster placement. He is a tiny newborn. Of course, our adoptions of Elijah, Kentrell, and Gabbi are final and Annabelle is eighteen months old. So, our new addition makes five kids in the house. We had been providing respite for this little guy, and when asked if he could stay, Richard said it was my decision since I am the primary caregiver. I sent one of our friends, Emily Goodman, who had become especially attached to our new guy a text.

Me—"DHR asked us to take the baby. Richard says it is my decision will you pray about it."

Emily—"I will pray about it. But you need to know that I have been praying that God will put him with people that will love him and teach him to love God. This may be an answer to my prayer! I love you and Richard and your willingness to love other people's children. I will be praying for you all."

First, that took the breath out of me. How could this not be an answer to Emily's prayer? We don't always get answers to prayers immediately but this was pretty fast. My mother-in-law told us after the adoption of our big kids that it was an emotional day because their prayer of twenty years had been answered. They had provided Richard and Laura with permanency in hopes that they would someday be able to commit to a spouse and children. Richard obviously is married and now has adopted three wonderful children from foster care. So, our prayers are not always answered immediately, but they are all heard and answered. Second, I never thought of it this way until Emily's text, but I truly believe her words, "your willingness to love other people's children" is my God given gift. So many people say they cannot do foster care, but my biggest thing is that they just need someone to love them. They need a home, a bed, and love. It breaks my heart to know that there are children sitting at DHR in the middle of the night while workers desperately call looking for them a home, and this trumps all the reasons why I can't do this. I don't have rose-colored glasses. I know that we cannot save every child, but maybe we can make a small impact. So, there will be heart ache and trials, obstacles and hurdles, but at least while a child is in foster care, I know that I can provide a warm bed, food, and a house full of love. And they are full of love to give! If foster care is not something you can do, there are so many other ways to help. Our families and church family support us and pray for us. They took care of us like no other while Richard was deployed. If you had told me that Richard was going to deploy and I would be pregnant at the time, that our best friends would move an hour away, that we would move houses weeks before deployment, would I/we have taken three foster children? Probably not. But God's plans are greater than ours. It was a blessing to be busy during Richard's deployment. I was still working, so between work and taking care of the kids, I was too tired to sit around, worrying or having a pity party.

God is all knowing and all powerful. Time and again, we see that God can see the big picture, and we cannot at times. We saw this in our miscarriages and deployment. This week, Ray and Pat Brown e-mailed Richard their portion for this book. In it, as you have read, they tell of a man named Van Ingram and the impact he had in their lives and ultimately he was responsible for bringing them to Huntsville to work with Memorial Parkway church of Christ and to become Richard's foster parents. Now about thirty years later, Richard and I are foster parents in Opelika, Alabama, and so are our friends Andrew and April Click. They actually attended our last foster parenting class as our guest because they were interested in becoming foster parents. Andrew is the grandson of Van Ingram. I had no idea this connection existed until this week and found it really neat and amazing and how God works in our lives.

Pepa Oden told us after the adoptions that he understood God's love for us when he met Gabbi the first time and he said, "I loved her instantaneously and knew that she was my

59

granddaughter." I think Pepa is right, and I feel that God blessed me with this amazing gift to love other people's children instantaneously to help Richard on his journey to pay it forward.

Brittany Oden

Thank you, babe, for so willingly coming on this journey with me to pay it forward. I love you so much!

CHAPTER 7

Giants Defeated

Some people have asked me and, at times, I would even ask myself, if I could change anything in my past—being a foster kid, sleeping in the back of cars, and the like—would I? When I was younger, my gut reaction was absolutely, but now that I am older, absolutely not. My whole life is the providence of God. I would not change a thing because that would mean changing the plan God had for me in my life. I would like to make this clear right now at this point in my book. This is not a "brag on Richard by Richard" book. I am very proud of where I am now at this point in my life because of where I came from, but *I give all the glory to God!* He is my Lord and Savior, and without Him and His providence in my life, my story and this book would not be possible. *Thank you, God, for being the loving God you are. My prayer is that many people will seek and find You because they read this book. Especially, thank You for the people You sent in my life, especially my wife. I love You!*

All my life I have felt like I was facing a Philistine (David and Goliath in the Bible, 1 Samuel 17:1–58). You see, as a foster child, I would sometimes be told or, most of the time, I would overhear, as it were, "That kid doesn't have a chance. He won't amount to anything." I guess, after hearing that time after time, some kids would start buying into that. I, on the other hand, turned that negative talk into positive motivation. My attitude was, "I'll show you and the world that this kid, although dealt a bad hand that he had no control over, could be a productive member of society and so much more." Let us remember who won that fight. 1 Samuel 17:50 reads, "So David prevailed over the Philistine with a sling and a stone, and struck the Philistine and killed him. But there was no sword in the hand of David." I think the people who know me would say that I have a desire to succeed that is hard to rival. Out of the ten kids my biological mom had, I was one of a few who graduated high school and, as far as I know, the only one to graduate college. Also, I am the first and only one out of the kids of my adopted family to graduate college although my sister is getting real close. You go, girl! Breaking the cycle can be very hard to do, but it can be done! People ask me if I drink, and my answer is always the same. I tell them the last time I had a drink was thirty-two years ago and I am only thirty-one. You can do the math. Of course, as each year goes by, I add one to those numbers. The next question is why I don't drink. I tell them I have two reasons why. They are my biological mom and dad. Both of them struggled with alcohol, and in turn, I believe that it has cost me a lot. If I never take that first drink then that cycle stops with me. Alcohol will not cost me any more hurt or sadness in my life. Praise God!

Before we got married Brittany and I went to premarriage counseling, like many other couples do and should. We talked a lot about our plans as related to finance, family, faith, and plans for children one day. We, or more likely, I decided that we should wait ten years after we were married to start our family. Well, like so many other plans, this one did not work out exactly like I planned. It was after about nine years when she came to me with a pregnancy test. Ready or not, it was positive. My first words were, "How did this happen?" Oh yeah, duh. After my initial shock, I was really excited, but nervous at the same time. I knew that I would make some mistakes and not be the perfect dad, but I also knew, if nothing else, I would be there for my children unlike my biological father. As you can imagine due to my biological father not being there in my life, I always felt like I had a part of me missing, unfortunately, like so many families in America today. So because I knew what that felt like, I would, at least, be there for mine. Thanks, biological father! I really mean that, not sarcastically. I really mean thank-you. I know now how important having a father around is and that's thanks to you.

My Full Life Circle, Squared—the title I chose, is especially appropriate. It comes from the fact that I was a foster kid, then became a foster parent (the first circle) and, for the second circle, the fact that I was adopted out of foster care and, Lord willing, will be adopting three of my foster kids. Now, for the rest of the story, as they say.

Unfortunately, early in this pregnancy, Brittany miscarried. We were hurt, but at the same time, we were thankful it was very early. No one ever wants a miscarriage, but if it has to happen, I think it hurts a little bit less if it is early. A year or so before this pregnancy, we had taken classes to get our foster care license. I just wanted to pay it forward. It was my calling. Our plan was to foster first, then start our family in that order. At first, we were affiliated with Agape of Montgomery, Alabama. I wanted to do Agape out of Huntsville because, as you know, that's who I was affiliated with when I was a foster kid, but we are geographically to far away. Like I said before, they had the same name, but they were different entities. Later we realized that being licensed with Agape of Montgomery was just not working out for us or them. One reason was it was more than an hour's drive from our house to their office, so Brittany and I decided to switch our license to Lee County DHR (Auburn-Opelika). A few months later, we got pregnant again. We were excited, but also very nervous, and we prayed a lot. A lot of couples will wait until the first trimester is successfully over to start telling people, but not me. I am a man of faith, so my theory was if no one knows early, how can they pray early? Although at first, my wife was cautious about this, she agreed. So we told people we were pregnant and asked them to pray that this time it would work. Unfortunately, this pregnancy did not work either. Now some might say my strategy did not work, and two months later the fact that this pregnancy did not work proves it. I will humbly tell them what I told my wife. Everything happens for a reason. It's not in our time, but it's in God's time. We can't argue with God. God has a plan for us. Yes, we may hurt and question why or what it is, but we must remain faithful and trust that His will be done, and His plan will be revealed. At this point, Brittany went to a special doctor in Montgomery to see what was going on. She had surgery and the doctors found that she had endometriosis. The surgery went fine and the doctors were very optimistic. My heart goes out to couples who can't get pregnant. Let me encourage you as well. Continue to read this book. You will see that God had a plan for us and He has one for you. It may be that He wants you to read this book and take that leap of faith with him to be a foster/adoptive parent yourself. So, our problem was carrying the child. Our doctor told us to wait a while and try again, and so we did, and we got pregnant again. At this point, we were walking on eggshells. We prayed a lot, and we asked people to pray, a lot. Yes, this was our third pregnancy, and yes, it happened again—three miscarriages! We were devastated but at the same time, we were faithful. We truly believed that God did, indeed, have a plan for us, and therefore, we refused to turn our backs on Him. We remained faithful. This was sometime in February 2013, and on April 25 of that same year, the phone rang. It was DHR asking if we could take two kids, a fourteen-month-old little girl and a two-year-old little boy, and of course, we said yes.

CHAPTER 8

Kick-Off Time

Brittany and I were like any other licensed want-to-be foster parents. We were well trained and ready. But you never know how you will do on game day until it's time to play, and the ref blows the kickoff whistle at Bryant-Denny Stadium. We were excited and nervous at the same time. So, on April 25, 2013, my first circle was complete in my full life circle, squared. I started out as a foster child and became a foster parent. They were and are two of the most beautiful children ever, and yes, I might be just a little partial. Brittany and I had to drive about thirty minutes from our house to get the kids from the other foster home where they were staying. This particular home asked for older kids, not babies, and as you probably have guessed, being that she was twenty-eight and I was thirty at the time, we wanted babies. So DHR saw fit to let us keep these little ones. After visiting the other foster mom, we put them in the car seats and drove toward home. That first night, we took them to meet our neighbors, which also happened to be our best friends, the Day family.

CHAPTER 9

One Special Day, or Four

Speaking of the Day family, the story of how God brought us so close together is nothing short of God's miraculous work. I think the story is pretty unbelievable, but believe it because it is true. I am a people person, so while I am at church, one of my many lines is, "So how is life treating you?" It was a Sunday morning and I asked Jeremy that very question. To my surprise, Jeremy said, "Well, Richard, it's just hard putting food on the table right now." At this point, Jeremy was working and finishing his engineering degree at Auburn University, and his wife just had a newborn baby boy. When he said this, it somewhat caught me off guard. Normally, the response I would get back from everybody I ask is, "Fine, what about you?" So I asked, and he told me, and our conversation ended. He was in no way asking for any kind of help. The vibe of the conversation I was getting was that he was just venting, like we all sometimes do and need to do. That night, however, I told my wife about this conversation and asked her if there was anything we could do. So, we talked about it and prayed about it, and we came up with the amount of three hundred dollars. We did not want the Days to know who this money came from for a couple of different reasons. First, if I were in Jeremy's shoes, I would want to pay back the money that was given to me if I knew where it came from. Two, if they knew, we would get some of the glory, and we felt like it was God who had blessed us with our finances, and therefore, He should get all the glory. So, we waited a little while after the conversation took place so, hopefully, they wouldn't figure it out. Well, about the time we were ready to make our move, an unexpected bill came in the mail, like they sometimes do, which was about—yep, you guessed it—three hundred dollars. So at this point, we talked about it and prayed some more. Both Brittany and I agreed that, yes, it would have been nice to take care of that unexpected bill, but we needed to put God first and go ahead with our plan and give the money we had already committed to Him. Our plan was to put the money in an envelope, give it to some of our friends at church, and ask them to put it directly into their hands and tell them it wasn't from them, but the people it came from wished to remain anonymous, and that was exactly what happened. A little while later, we were carpooling with the Day family on our way to Columbus, Georgia, close to an hour's drive from where we lived in Opelika, to see a newborn baby and family at the hospital who attended our church. Of course, it was Jeremy and me in the front seat and the two girls and the newborn baby boy in the back. On our drive, Jeremy said, "Richard, something really neat happened to me at church. It was good, but I really don't know what to do about it." I said, "What's that?" He proceeded to tell me that he was handed an envelope that had *three hundred dollars* in it. The reason I italicized *three hundred dollars* in this last line is to try to show you that he was astonished that it had this much in it. Anyways, he went on to tell me that he really wanted to thank the people it came from, but he did not know how because he did not know who it came from. At this point, as you can imagine, the hairs on the back of my neck stood straight up, and I got goose bumps. In my mind I was thinking, *Wow, God! What a blessing it is to do your work and be your people, and thank You so much for blessing me with this very moment.* To know that He (God) blessed the very people in the car riding next to us and used us to do that and Jeremy thanking us without him knowing, it was us who gave him the envelope.

Wow, what a moment! I told him whoever it was who gave him the envelope knew he was thankful for it and to not try to figure it out, "because if they wanted you to know, they would have told you." He agreed, and I also told him that later, if I were in his shoes, I would pay that blessing forward if I could. He agreed to that as well, and we went on talking about something else. So, we invested a measly three hundred dollars, which we almost decided not to, in God's work, and in return, He blessed us with our very best friends in the world. You know the ones—if you ever need anything you could call them, and no matter what it was, they would be there! To my knowledge Jeremy and Beth Day still don't know who gave them that envelope, and I guess, the only way they will figure it out is if they read this book. I, at first, wasn't going to put this story in this book, but a roommate of mine, who turned into a close friend, airman first class Zack Stettler, while we were deployed to Afghanistan, told me that this story had to go in my book. The reason I told him was that you can't out give God, and of course, I used this story as my example, but the story does not end there. As if the Day family becoming our best friends wasn't enough, soon after, they signed a one-year lease to live in one of our rental houses which they ended up staying in for close to three years. That house was in the same circle as the one we lived in, two doors down! I cut him a deal at six hundred dollars a month. I did do the math and my physical return on investment that the Lord blessed us with was sixty-eight times the original amount of the three hundred dollars. They were great tenants, not to mention our best friends living two doors down. I say again, *you can't outgive God!* Try it. I challenge you! As a matter of fact, God himself challenges you too in Malachi 3:10, and I quote, "Bring all the tithes into the storehouse, That there may be food in my house, and try me now in this, says the Lord of hosts, If I will not open for you the windows of heaven and pour out for you such blessing that there will not be room enough to receive it." In the NIV[4], which I like a lot better, it says, "Bring the whole tithe into the storehouse, that there may be food in my house. Test me in this," says the Lord Almighty, "and see if I will not throw open the floodgates of heaven and pour out so much blessing that there will not be room enough to store it." This, by the way, is the only place in the whole Bible that God tells us to test Him. I have done this and have tried to paint this picture through these words in this book. If God has blessed me, like I ask Him to in the second paragraph of this book, then you can see, He has done exactly what He said for me in Scripture, and He will do the same for you. *Keep His promises.* Keep in mind, the Lord uses the word *blessings*, not necessarily *money*. This might include money, but it might not, and it also would include health, opportunity, and others. Jeremy and Beth, we love you guys so much. Thank you for being the people that you are—God's people. As stated already, you and God have paid us back a million fold. I hope it's not awkward the next time we see you after you have read this book. We love you and your sweet little babies who we claim as our first babies. Also, if you haven't already, remember what I told you on that faithful day in the car on our way to Columbus, Georgia. Pay it forward. I really look forward to hearing you tell that story and hearing how God, in return, has blessed you as He did us! I know you will, and God will! Thanks again for everything. We *love you*!

The Days have two children close to Gabbi and Kentrell's age—at this point, a little girl and boy as well. It was sad to see my two foster babies so excited over the Day babies' insignificant little toys. It really put it in perspective for my wife, Jeremy and Beth, but not for me. You see, when I moved, as stated before, I packed all my belongings in a single black plastic garbage bag. When my babies

---

4   The Hold Bible, New International Version®; Grand Rapids; Zondervan House, 1984.

came into our care, they didn't even have a bag. That night was very emotional for me and my wife. We knew in those moments that God put me in foster care so I could relate better to my babies, who are in my foster home, more than anyone else in foster care. I often wonder when the foster care license application asks the question, "Why do you want to be a foster/adoptive parent?" how many people can say, "because I was a foster kid, and I was adopted?" I would imagine very few. As stated before, I had a calling, and I wanted to pay it forward, but most of all, I wanted to show these children what a home and family were supposed to be like; a home with a mother and a father who had God and the Bible at the center of their lives; a home that would teach them who God was and why we should follow Him; a home that would love them unconditionally; a home that had peace because of the Prince of Peace, and a home just like so many that I lived in. In 2 Timothy 3:16–17 it states, "All scripture is given by inspiration of God and is profitable for doctrine, for reproof, for correction, for instruction in righteousness, that the man of God may be complete, thoroughly equipped for every good work." That first night, after we put Gabbi and Kentrell down, Brittany and I were lying in bed, winding down, as you can imagine, and as already stated before, this particular day carried with it a lot of nerves, anxiety, and emotions. While lying there, I asked her, "Honey, if any of the first three pregnancies worked, would we have told DHR yes when they called and asked us about Gabbi and Kentrell?" We both decided that if we had a newborn, then we would have told them no.

CHAPTER 10

Our New Life

Over the first few weeks, both of the kids were great, with absolutely no problems. We didn't even miss any sleep! Wow, they call this the honeymoon stage, of course.

When we had the kids about two weeks or so, we started taking them to day care. It was my job to take them. On the first day, when I loaded them up, Kentrell asked, "Where are we going?" One would believe this is a normal question for a little boy Kentrell's age, and it was. However, every other time we got in the car the same question came up, and I started thinking about it. Was this, in fact, just a curious two-year-old or was there more to it? Then it hit me—one of the reasons they came into foster care was they were left at home by themselves, so they probably didn't get to ride in the car that much.

After about the fourth week, Brittany came to me and said, "Kentrell started crying when I put him to bed, and I don't know why." I told her, "I do." I went in his room and asked him what was wrong, and he said, "Nothing" in a two-year-old baby's voice. I said, "You miss your mommy, don't you?" Keep in mind that this little boy's world just got turned upside down, and at even at two years old, being in our house, even if it was a million times better than where he came from, it was not what he knew. I explained, "Baby, when I was a little boy just like you, I got taken away from my mommy, and I missed my mommy too, and that is okay. Anytime you want to talk about it we can." He said, "OK." I gave him a big hug and put him back in bed. To this day, over a year later, we haven't had the same problem. The providence of God, as I have been trying to show you in this book, was clear. God, indeed had a plan for me—us. There is no doubt in my mind that God put me in foster care so I could minister to those like me later down the road, and that later came with Gabbi, Kentrell, and their five-year-old brother, Elijah!

Yes, we are crazy, and yes, we took another of their siblings. Elijah was four when we first met him. Brittany and I threw Kentrell a huge backyard birthday bash. We invited the entire sibling group and their biological mom. We thought it would give their biological mom an opportunity to visit all five of her kids who were in foster care, without doing so in a boring DHR conference room. To our disappointment, but not necessarily to our surprise, all her kids showed up but their biological mom must have had something better to do. After telling us she would be there, she was a no call, no show. Elijah spent most of the party with my parents that day. He fixed his plate and plopped down with Nana and Papa, and they were instant friends. That night, I told my wife I wanted Elijah. He was and is the sweetest little boy, and with some of daddy's (me) tough and tender love, he too could come to know and follow God, and we could help him with that. I also said he needed a positive father figure just like I did when I was his age. Brittany was somewhat mad at me for even bringing it up. We had already taken in two small kids and just the thought of another—well, let's just say, I was lucky to make it through the night alive. So, because I'm me and I am stubborn, I already made up my mind about Elijah. I just had to figure out a way to make her mind up, too. Not too long after that we got a phone call from our social worker telling us that the foster mom keeping Elijah had requested immediate removal of him from her home. This home was a single mom who had three children of her own as well as the other three siblings of our kids. Brittany and I talked about it again, and we decided that we did not want the siblings to get split up more than they already were. We agreed to take Elijah. By the way, I believe that the way this all worked out was no coincidence. I truly believe that this was God's providence working in Elijah's life. When we told our parents, some disapproved of the way they felt DHR pressured us to take Elijah. I humbly told them that the way it worked out did not matter. What did matter was that Elijah now lived with us, he had a positive father figure, and he had a better opportunity to come to know God. Later, I was talking with Elijah and I said, "You know, son, the first time I met you, I wanted you to come live with us. Why don't you go ask your mother (Brittany) if that's true?" So he did, and she said, "Yes, Elijah, the first time Daddy met you, he wanted you to live with us." Then to be funny, I told him to ask if Mommy felt the same way the first time she met him. He did. She gave me the death stare and changed the subject, and yes, I stay in trouble with Brittany, but that's one of the reasons I love her so much. She puts up with me!

Now we had three out of the five siblings. All three thrived in our house. Elijah was the most affectionate of my boys. He loves giving and receiving hugs and kisses. He and his Nana (my mom) hit it off from day one at Kentrell's birthday party. Gabbi had me wrapped in a matter of days, and Kentrell—well; don't get me wrong, Kentrell is a sweet little boy. Let's just say he shows the potential to be a really fun teenager, if you know what I mean. Sometimes when you ask him to do something, he would just sit there and stare at you. This would really get under our skin, so we would make him stand in the corner. We told him why it was important to do things the first time he was asked. A few months after we got Elijah, we found out we were pregnant again. No, this one was not planned. I remember telling my dentist office about it and one of them saying, "Wow, with three little ones, I'm surprised you guys had time for all that." She was trying to make me blush, not an easy task. I said, "People find time to do things that are important to them" and "Life is good!" Touché! We prayed and tried not to get our hopes up too high, but still, as stated before, we believed that God had a plan for us. At this exact moment, May 7 at three in the morning in Bagram, Afghanistan, Brittany is in Alabama at work on May 6 in the afternoon carrying our unborn baby girl, Annabelle Elizabeth Oden. The doc told us on Friday (the one before I was to leave for my deployment) that Brittany was through the first trimester and was doing great. At this same appointment, we confirmed that the baby was a girl, and yes, I did use the word *confirm*. You see, I have told people, since before we started trying to have children, that the male parent, as scientists would say, decides the gender of the baby, and I decided it was a girl. When my father-in-law asked what the baby was, and Brittany told him, he said, "*Oh, no!* We will never hear the end of this from Richard." I thought that was pretty funny.

Brittany and I strongly felt that God's plan was revealed to us. Remember when I asked her if any of the previous pregnancies had worked out and DHR called us, would we have said yes to keeping our babies and our answer would have been no—not with a newborn. Well, God knew that, and this was His plan. He wanted us to get Gabbi, Kentrell, and Elijah; then and only then, would He bless us with baby Annabelle. It's like I said before, "In His time, not ours; In His order, not ours. It's His will, not ours!" In Ecclesiastes 3:1 it is said, "To everything there is a season, a time for every purpose under heaven."

No corporal punishment is the rule for all foster homes in the state of Alabama. This means that foster parents cannot spank, pop, or do, anything physical to a child in care. Because of the no corporal punishment rule in the state of Alabama, Brittany and I feel like we are trying to raise our kids with one hand behind our backs. I understand, in some cases, there shouldn't be any, but to make it across the board like it is, we don't agree with that at all. And no, the no corporal punishment law is not in every state. Having said that, we have never second-guessed our decision to become foster parents.

You know what the rules are before the children are placed with you. Also, we knew that this was a worthwhile undertaking, and anything as important as this we knew would not be easy, but it is so worth it!

So, here we were a white couple with three African-American babies. I will say when we took them out in public we got a lot of strange looks. However, we also had a lot of people stop and talk to us who normally wouldn't have. After having Gabbi and Kentrell for a little while we invited their biological mom to church then to lunch at our house afterwards. To our pleasant surprise, she came to both! This was a really neat experience, to say the least. We got the opportunity to know her and find out her story. She was also a foster child and grew up in the North part of the country—same old story, and the cycle continues.

CHAPTER 11

Life Isn't Fair

One of our goals as their foster parents, even if we don't get to adopt them, is to instill in them the fact that life isn't fair. Every time I hear one of mine say, "That's not fair," I immediately say, "Hey! Are you in foster care?"

"Yes, Daddy."

"Is that fair?"

"No, Daddy."

"So what do we do about that?"

"We get over it, and we move on."

Then I tell them that I love them. I know that may seem a little harsh, but I think I am more than qualified to make this statement. I tell them I expect them to be productive members of society. I'm not asking them to do or be anything extraordinary, but of course, if they want to be, I would support them one hundred percent. But then again, if these children would only do what I am asking and become productive members of society, then that would mean that they did break the vicious cycle, and that is extraordinary. In not so many words, I am teaching them not to let their past define their future. It is not easy to do. I realize that. However, if I can do it, so can these kids and any kids. While their biological mom was at our house we asked her if she or her friends had a problem with us being white. She did admit that some of her friends gave her some flack because of it. We proceeded to tell her that we would train her kids to see as God sees. God is color-blind and therefore, we should be too. She said she was fine with that. Another neat thing about her visit was that she got to put her eyes on where her kids lived, their environment, their bedrooms, and she helped us put them down for their nap. I don't know how long it had been since she had done that or if she ever had, but she did it the way we did, our routine, and that was to simultaneously sing and rock them to sleep. After her visit we were very confident that she had nothing to worry about when it came to Gabbi and Kentrell. She got to see firsthand the love we had for her babies. Later, she confirmed what I had said about her worrying about her kids whom we had. She told us that she knew her kids were truly loved in our home and that they were spoiled rotten. That was truly a blessing to hear her say those words! Being cordial with their biological mom is a true blessing as well! I remember the first time I met their biological mom. I told her she was doing a lot more than my biological mom did when it was time to get us back. She got very emotional.

Mother's Day 2014

It is Mother's Day here in Bagram, Afghanistan, May 12, 2014. We got attacked by four or five rockets last night, and they put us on lockdown, so Mom, I did not forget to call you. Happy Mother's Day. I love you.

CHAPTER 12

Special Moments

As stated before, being cordial with their biological mom is a blessing but we sometimes have anxiety when a situation presents itself—like when her kids call us Mom and Dad around her. But, for the most part, it has been great. We told her we would like to adopt her children and to our surprise—at that time, anyway—she agreed that it would probably be for the best. However, because her older two children were in a foster home as well (one that was not going to adopt them), she would not sign the TPR paperwork. I told her that she would always be welcome to see her kids if we did, adopt them or even while they were our foster babies. Remember, I was in her kids' shoes and that's what I would have wanted.

Speaking of uncomfortable situations; Brittany and I threw Gabbi and Elijah a combined birthday party at our church building. Gabbi was turning two and Elijah was turning five. We invited both sides of our family and their biological mom. The kids and I went to pick their biological mom and there were a few moments of awkward silence that occurred. However, it didn't last too long—thank goodness—and we started talking about different things. When we arrived at the church building their biological mom and her three kids all got to jump in the big bouncing blow-up house we rented for the party. It was neat seeing them spend that fun time together. Later, as more people started coming, a moment happened that I will never forget. Brittany was standing on the right talking to their biological mom who was standing on the left. The next thing I saw was two-year-old Gabbi running up directly in the middle of the two ladies saying, "Mommy, Mommy, Mommy." At this point two things were going through my head: first, man, was this awkward, and two, *Come on, Gabbi Girl, make a right fork toward Brittany*, and she did! I played it off as best I could, but in my mind I was yelling, *Yes, Gabbi Girl, I love you so much!* Their biological mom played it off pretty good, or it just didn't bother her. Remember earlier, when I said there were moments that occurred with your foster kids that made it all worth it, this was yet another example. Another example would be when I rocked Gabbi to sleep at night. It started with just me singing along with the iPad the song "Special to Me" by Martha's Trouble (a great record for little ones, by the way). Eventually, little two-year-old Gabbi would chime in and out of the song with us. The chorus of the song goes, "You're so special, you're so special to me, you're so special, you're so special to me," then I would add her name Gabbi because it was her name, and it rhymed. One night, we started our routine; first we pray, then I rock and sing her to sleep. This night she was chiming in more than usual, so I wanted to see how much she would sing by herself. When the chorus began, I stopped and listened. My little two-year-old Gabbi sang, and I quote, "YOU'RE SO SPECIAL, YOU'RE SO SPECIAL, YOU'RE SO SPECIAL TO ME, DADDY." Instead of her name, Gabbi, she added my name, Daddy. That night, I went to my wife with tears in my eyes and told her what had happened, and I said, "No matter if we get to adopt these children or not, no matter how much heartbreak or come what may, this made it all worth it!" I have no doubt in my mind that some of you who are reading this book are thinking about being that special family to do something many people won't do and take that leap of faith with God and become foster/adoptive parents. God will bless you with moments like these with your foster/adoptive kids and it will, indeed, make it all worth it!

So now let us talk about my second circle in my full life circle, squared. In order to complete this circle, I would have to officially adopt my three foster babies, and if not these, heaven forbid, then some in the future. This is where you, as my readers, come in. I need your help. What can I do, you might ask. First and foremost, pray that the adoption goes through, then suggest to all around you to read this book and ask them to pray as well. I would like the prayers to bombard the Lord's door every moment of the day, 24-7. If the adoption goes through by the time you or they read this book, then pray for any and all foster/adoptive kids and parents. You see, as the song states, all kids need to feel like they are so special, but especially foster/adoptive kids.

Our Tenth Anniversary

Today, May 22, 2014, is our tenth wedding anniversary; well, today in Bagram. Afghanistan, where I am. Brittany, back home, has several more hours before it is the same date there in the States. We will FaceTime over a candlelit dinner—not exactly what we had in mind ten years prior, but hey, it's better than being deployed on your tenth anniversary before the Internet and technology today. I usually get her flowers, but this year, I got her Edible Arrangements—you know, the fruit and stuff that are made to look like flowers, and you can eat them. My thinking was this would be something for Brittany and Annabelle and the kids to enjoy. If she didn't like this—the chances of that are pretty good when I get bright ideas—then her birthday was right around the corner, and I could make it up to her then. *Happy anniversary, babe! I love you!*

CHAPTER 13

Deployment Time

About a year or so after we got the kids, it was time for my deployment. I am a UPS driver in my civilian life, and as already stated, I am a member of the 187th Fighter Wing, which is an Air National Guard unit in Montgomery, Alabama, where I am an F-16 crew chief. Brittany and I did everything we could to help the kids try to understand this. I think our five-year-old Elijah was somewhat getting it, but not the other two. In a way, I felt bad. I mean, one of our many goals was to stop the revolving door of people they get attached to coming in and out of their lives. Remember, I know exactly what that feels like, and know I was one of them; however, I know that this is different. I just pray that if the adoption does not go through, then my babies won't leave until I get home from my six-month deployment to Bagram. If that happens and they must go, then I would really like a chance to say good-bye, so you – I – we pray!

I am really excited about my deployment and, yes, nervous too. You see, there are many reasons people join the military—a steady job, education benefits, VA benefits, and honor, just to name a few. Every single one of these reasons is really good, but for me, I would fall under the last one I mentioned. God had already blessed me with a really good job with really good benefits, which included paying for most of my college, which I had already completed when I enlisted. Serving in the military had always been a dream of mine. I wanted so badly to get my flags—you know the one they put over your coffin when you die; the one they fly in front of your gravestone; and the one they fold up and give to your wife or family at the graveside. After I graduated high school, I was a signature away from signing with the navy, but my virtuous wife—or girlfriend at the time, said, "Ah, I'm not sure about that," so I waited. Brittany had never been really keen on my military dream. After about ten years of asking, practically begging her, and telling her that I was 28 years old, and before too long, the military would not take me because I would be too old, she said, "Well, if that's what you really want to do, then who am I to stop you?" After she said that, I went and enlisted as fast as I could before she could change her mind! When I signed with the Air National Guard, I got my flags, and now, at age 31, while on my deployment, I am earning them!

Let me take a second and talk to all kids—especially foster, adoptive ones. For some, you might have had a rough life, and if you are in foster care and you didn't get adopted and age out of the foster care system when you turn eighteen, then it's out on your own; good luck. I would urge you to consider joining the military. This would give you structure, discipline, a steady job, a roof over your head, food, and many other benefits including an opportunity to go to college, and pride, knowing that you are serving your country. I can't think of a better place to work, for that would give someone who has had a rough life all that opportunity. I do understand your fears. I might get deployed, and I might die. Yes, you might, but you might be on your way to the store and get in a car wreck and die. Everyone dies. The main point is to be prepared. Life on earth is temporary, but eternity is forever. Make sure you know where you want to spend eternity, and do what you must to get there. There are many jobs that the military offers. Some are a lot less dangerous than others. Do your research. You might be surprised at what the military has to offer.

There we were with the three little ones and my wife expecting. The baby was due on September 24, 2014, and I was not scheduled to get home until November 8, 2014. You can do the math. So what in the world did we do, you might ask; I addressed the congregation at Tenth Street church of Christ, in Opelika, Alabama, where we attended. I thanked them for immediately taking our babies in as part of the church family and also thanked them for coming up to Brittany and telling her to call if she needed anything while I was away. I went on to say how nice that was, but nobody wants to feel like a burden, and I knew my wife—she would not call. I then asked them to take that to the next level, to go the extra mile—like the Bible tells us to in Matthew 5:41, "And whoever compels you to go one mile, go with him two" —to be creative and do things like just showing up and asking, "What do you need?" and not take no or nothing for an answer or maybe keeping the kids so she could run some errands or have a little 'me time'. Brittany would, no doubt, have her hands full, but I had no worries when I left, for I knew that God's people would do God's work as we are commanded in Galatians 6:9–10, "And let us not grow weary while doing good, for in due season we shall reap if we do not loose heart. Therefore, as we have opportunity, let us do good to all, especially to those who are of the household of faith." I knew that they would do exactly that and take care of my family while I was deployed.

Today, May 31, 2014, is my thirty-second birthday. I got an award that stated, "In appreciation for your sacrifice and spending your birthday in a combat zone, with three hundred of your closest friends in Bagram, Afghanistan, for Operation Enduring Freedom. We say thank you and happy birthday!" I am proud to do what so many before me have done and so many after me will do. And that is to put service before self, which happens to be one of three of the Air Force's core values. The other two being integrity first and excellence in all we do, by which I also strive to live by.

CHAPTER 14

Action vs. Words

Being that I'm a foster parent and in the military, I have a lot of people thanking me and Brittany for what we do for the kids and, when I'm in uniform, a lot of people thanking me for my service to this great country. I often wonder if that is as far as it goes. These words are nice, but as we all have heard about what actions do when it comes to words, and I quote, "Actions speak louder than words." Do people stop and think about the real and significant sacrifices that we (foster parents and/or members of our military and their families) make? I'm missing my birthday, my wife's birthday, my child's birthday, our ten-year anniversary, Mother's Day, and my first Father's Day, not to mention the birth of our firstborn child. These dates are times that we will never get back. On the foster care side, we sacrifice our needs and wants, just like any other good traditional parent should. For our kids, we leave our hearts vulnerable because just like signing up for the military, we know what could happen, and yet we still go! So let me take a few moments to encourage you to encourage foster parents and our military members. Do what I asked my church to do—go the extra mile, and let them know how much you appreciate them. I have a lady at my church who has given me a total of forty dollars. I try to refuse it, but she insists. She says that when she sees a military member at the airport, she wants them to know how much she appreciates what they do and the sacrifices that they make so she can lay her head down at night and feel safe. She says she wants to buy them lunch, and she has for me twice—first when I left for basic training and second when I left for Afghanistan. Because of her and because I too want to pay this forward, I thought of a neat thing I will do; maybe you can do the same. The next time I'm in the airport in my civilian clothes and I see a member of our military, I will go up and thank them for their service and ask them if I can buy their lunch and not take no for an answer, then get their name and tell them that they will be in our family's nightly prayers until their mission is over. For foster parents, do some of the same things I asked my church to do as well. Tell the foster parents that you are coming over to keep the kids so the foster parents can have a date night; again, like I asked my church, be creative with your actions, and show both military members and foster/adoptive parents that you really do appreciate what they're doing. Take it from me; all these things really help. You just might be giving them the encouragement they need to keep carrying on. To those military families who have paid the ultimate sacrifice, I realize that everything I mentioned was minute in comparison to what you have sacrificed. *Thank you so much!*

Now I want to tell you what my Mema and Pepa wrote about having three and four jobs while going to and graduating college. After I graduated high school, I started my own lawn care business. I called it College Help Lawn Care, and my slogan was, "Not only could you get your lawn cut, but you could also help out a young man trying to get his college education." My customers really liked the idea that they were getting a good service, and at the same time, they were investing in my future, so I did pretty well. College Help Lawn Care gave me the opportunity to meet and talk to many different people. Little did I know that I would meet and maintain a close friendship with a sweet couple who were customers of mine. Their names are Les and Patricia Potter. I have asked them to say a few words. This is what they wrote:

I met Richard when he was nineteen because of his grass-cutting flyer in a mail box. Richard impressed my wife and me when we first met and hired him to cut our lawn while we were away on vacation. After returning from vacation, we continued his services until he got married and moved away. When he had some time available he would stay for a while (never more than half an hour), and talk with me about a very special lady (that became his wife), his history, his hopes for the future, his goals and a belief that he had to give back. That included helping others in the foster home system and a desire to give back to his nation as well. We were really impressed by a young man that had four jobs and was going to college full time.

He called me from a bus during part of his initial Air Force training just to tell me he had finally done it and enlisted as we had discussed years before. We have maintained contact over the years and look forward to a visit the next time Richard, Brittany, and the children are in town. I was aware of some information in this book from our conversations and friendship but found there was much more to Richard's history that hadn't been shared.

Les Potter

Thank you, Les and Patricia Potter, for all the encouragement over the years. Believe me when I say we really treasure our friendship with you. Les, your service as a Marine to this country as well as many veterans like you is why I wanted to serve as well. Thank you, and God bless!

As I was saying about my company College Help Lawn Co., I would not pull the car over for less than thirty dollars an hour. So in my mind, my friends and I made $7.25/hour bagging groceries. I knew I could make more than four times that much, cutting grass. Yes, I continued to work for Winn-Dixie, and one day while at Winn-Dixie, I started chatting with some soft-drink vendors. They told me they needed someone to stock their shelves on the weekends at about three or four local grocers in the area, and it paid about one hundred dollars a weekend, and so being me, I jumped right on that and got the job. So at this point, I had Pepsi, Winn-Dixie, and College Help Lawn Care, and then my mom came home and told me that a lady she worked with told her that her husband was a driver at UPS Inc., and they were hiring part-time people. I heard UPS Inc. was a great company to work for with great benefits, and they would even reimburse my college tuition if I made decent grades, so you know what I did.

Now keep in mind, this whole time, I was dating Brittany. My father-in-law-to-be made me the same deal that was made to him when he asked for the blessing from Brittany's mother's dad, his father-in-law-to-be then. The deal was I could marry her when I got my college degree. He did not, however, give me a time frame, so you know what I did? Yep, while working four part-time jobs, I also took classes at Calhoun Community College, then at my mom's alma mater, Athens State University in Athens, Alabama—spring, summer, and fall. I graduated with a double major in business administration and human resources management in three years. He did hold up his end of the bargain, and as you already know, we got married. I did not get a lot of sleep, but it was all worth it. I was still facing my Philistines of what people said when I was in foster care— of how they decided kids in foster care wouldn't amount to anything.

Not only did I graduate a year early, but as stated already, I was also the first one out of my biological parents' children and my adopted parents' children to graduate college. My in-laws, parents, Brittany, and God are to whom I give all the credit for that but, of course, all in the reverse order. About those jobs, owning my own business was the one that taught me the most. I always had the entrepreneur spirit. I always knew, one day, I wanted to own my own business, but I never thought it would be right out of high school—in God's time, not mine. Sometimes it comes early, sometimes it comes late, and other times, it does not come at all, but it is His will, not mine. Owning my own business taught me a whole lot more responsibility. Being your own boss is nice and I did make good money, but more than the money was the experience I treasured. I knew if I wanted to take a day off, then I would have to work twice as hard the next day, and if that next day rained, well, I was in a pickle, and the only one I could blame was myself. So I learned the hard way to plan ahead before I gave myself the day off. Live and learn—as a foster kid or foster parent, this principle is incredibly important. We all know, "The definition of *insanity* is doing something over and over again and expecting a different result."[5] Well, many people, me included, have been insane by definition. In life, be productive. Don't waste your time by doing this. If you mess up, try something different. If I were in your shoes, I would pray and ask God for His guidance and wisdom, then try something different, and then ask for other people for advice or help. For foster kids or for any kids or parents for that matter, don't do something because it is what everybody else is doing. Live by another life principle I live by: "Dare to change those around you, not to change into those around you." That applies to what people are doing, saying, thinking, or believing—like when people say, "That boy won't amount to anything" or when you are parents of

---

[5]   Albert Einstein; German physicist; (1879-1955).

four biological children and you tell your friends you want to adopt two foster kids, and they call you crazy. This principle is also going to be for sale under my business, Life Principle Tees LLC. The shirt will say, "Dare to change those around you, not to change into those around you!" Romans 12:2 says, "And do not be conformed to this world, but be transformed by the renewing of your mind, that you may prove what *is* that good and acceptable and perfect will of God."

CHAPTER 15

Arm Your Arsenal

You, your body, and your mind or mental state can handle more than you can think; high school football and the military taught me this. Being a foster parent, you will find that although you might be mentally and physically exhausted, you can bear a lot more than you can think. I would encourage you to face your Philistines; use your arsenal of tools to help you. If you don't have an arsenal, start one. My arsenal includes, first and foremost, my faith. I can't imagine going through what I have without my faith—from living with my biological mom, to foster care, to being adopted, to being a foster/adoptive parent, and to being deployed in a combat zone in Afghanistan. If you don't have faith, I strongly urge you to find some, and if you seek, you will find as we are promised in Matthew 7:7–8, "Ask, and it will be given to you; seek, and you will find; knock, and it will be opened to you. For everyone who asks receives, and he who seeks finds, and to him who knocks it will be opened." The first place to start is the Scriptures. I am a church of Christ, New Testament Christian, so that is what I recommend. I hope you can see what God has brought me through and how He has blessed me. With this, once you have found your faith, be all in; don't be lukewarm. Next is my best friend, which also happens to be my wife. If I get the wrong mind-set or if I have a bad attitude or have a question on a decision I am trying to make, she is that person I go to first, someone I can lean on, someone I can trust. Then in my arsenal would be my family and church family, somewhere I can go and ask for prayers, get words of encouragement, or vent, somewhere I can go and be served. One of my biggest problems for years, and I imagine I'm not the only one, is my pride. I would always be the one to serve but would not allow being served. If you do decide to be a foster parent, support and encouragement go a long way. A lot of foster parents find their support with other foster parents in the same county. In some counties, the support groups are even official, and you can add these to your arsenal as it grows. What Brittany and I have discovered, the longer you have the foster kids, the more people will want to help, and if they don't, you may need to find new friends. If this book gets you to start thinking about being a foster parent, these foster parent groups would be happy to have you come visit their get-togethers.

What you're about to read was, by far, the hardest thing for me to write. One of the many purposes of this book is to encourage people who may be thinking about becoming foster/adoptive parents to take that leap of faith with God and face their Philistines of the unknown, potential heartbreak, and what they may consider failure, so here we go. You can't save them all. In the classes you will take to get your foster care license, they tell you to know your limits. Yes, I have already written in this book that high school football and the military have taught me that my mental and physical limits were a lot more than I ever thought possible, but if you do reach the breaking point, call DHR, and do what needs to be done. I know this would be hard and that you would feel like you're throwing in the towel, but do it. Don't sacrifice your other kids, marriage, or relationship with God because, for example, you get a foster kid who requires all your time, attention, and effort. Keep in mind what I said—in God's time, not your time. Maybe the timing isn't right. God may want you to wait until your biological kids move out before you start foster care. Hopefully, you will not run into this kind of situation, so let's say you just need a short break. In the classes you will take, you will also learn about respite days; these are one of many benefits you will receive for being a foster parent. Respite days are days you have credit for where your foster kids can go to weekend foster parents so you and whoever can get away and have some me time. You can use these days for any reason; they are not guaranteed, but if you give DHR enough notice, then it usually isn't a problem, and they don't have to be used on the weekends, but they usually are. Foster parents are allowed a few respite days a year in the state of Alabama. In other states, I'm not sure, but now that you know what to ask for, ask. If you don't have these in your state, don't fret; there are always other options you could explore, like family, church family, and foster care charities. Foster parents are doing what many won't do, and there is a lot of support out there for you. If you need them, use them. Let them serve. That's what they are there for!

CHAPTER 16

Care Package

Today, June 12, 2014, in Bagram, Afghanistan, has been one of the best days I have had since I have been here! First, I got an unexpected package in the mail from a lady at church. This lady and her family were foster parents at one time. She kept our babies at her house so my wife could run some errands. While they were there, she took individual pictures with the three of them holding a chalkboard with three different things drawn on them. Elijah's board said "WE," sweet little Gabbi Girl's had a picture of a *heart*, and Kentrell's had a big *U*. Together it said, "WE <HEART> U" in a black-and-white photograph; it was awesome! Second, she sent me a book and a letter that said this book inspired her to become a foster parent. I was excited to read it because as you already know, that is one of my main goals in this book—to inspire people to open their homes and hearts to give good homes to desperate kids who need them so badly, like the author of the book she gave me, Ashley Rhodes-Courter, who wrote *Three Little Words*, and the author of this book, me. I have not been able to set it down. I have already read over half the book, and I just got it today. This is a big deal because this is only the second book I have ever read for pleasure, the first one being years ago while I was still in high school; it was *Gump & Co.*, the sequel to *Forrest Gump*. In her book, she covers some of the same issues I have written about in this book. I started to wonder if the lady from church would believe that I had already written in this book what the author wrote in her book before she sent it to me. But then I thought, well, even though Ashley and I have similar backgrounds, she had a lot worse foster care stint than I had, and the two books are completely different, just like our lives. But since we both lived in foster care, of course we would have some of the same questions and feelings. I feel like if I ever met her, then we would get along like long-lost friends would. It is my goal, after the event of the morning, to swap books with her face-to-face so she can have a signed copy of this book and for me to get at least two signed copies of hers—one for me and one for that lady at church! Second, today I got two more bomb lanyards! A bomb lanyard is a piece of wire that is attached to the bomb on the fighter jet. When a bomb is dropped, if the piece of wire remains on the jet, we know the bomb is active and not dud. To we military personnel, this is cherished war trophy. My aircraft 88-0399 dropped three out of its four bombs today and emptied its rounds in its big gun. The pilots saved lives with it today, and the pilot gave me two of the bomb lanyards, both of which I gave away—one to the airman who was in a different cell, but back home, aircraft 88-0399 was his baby and the other to my counterpart on the other shift. "Service before self," remember! As if that weren't enough, he blew over three Porta Johns while taxiing. I can't wait to see what that sticker looks like up against the bomb and the gun stickers that we put on the air-craft whenever it drops or fires! And if I know the guys, those Porta John stickers will appear even if just temporarily!

Okay, readers, it is June 13, 2014, and two "providence of God" things happened today. First, I asked one of my master sergeants to pray for my foster children—in particular, that it would not work out for one of the children's relative who lived in Michigan whom we were told had started taking foster care classes so they could keep our babies. This family, I think, had three of their own kids and wanted all the other five—our three and the other two. One of the things we were told was, they were asking about what the payments were going to be. I can't predict the future, but I knew that if they went back to Michigan, well, let's just say, the cycle would be primed and ready to rear its ugly head, and these babies—all babies—deserved better than that. So when I FaceTimed my wife this morning, she told me that that relative was not being cooperative, and it did not look like it was going to work out. These were words that she had been told by our caseworker, who had been contacted by the caseworkers in Michigan. Praise *God*! Next, that book that I told you about, which I started reading yesterday, sent by that lady from church—I am almost finished with it. I got to the part where Ashley filed a class action lawsuit against the state of Florida, and my jaw hit the floor. A month or so before my deployment, I had a package for a child advocate center, where they recruit and host foster care classes. I told the lady at the front desk that I wanted to talk to whoever was in charge. She thought it was for a complaint, but I just wanted to tell her that I was a foster kid and now a foster parent and that if she wanted me to speak on foster parent license graduation night, it would be my pleasure and that I had done the same thing for Lee County DHR, and I also spoke at the BigHouse Foundation, a foster and adoption charity, for a fund-raiser. The director had stepped out of the office, but the lady took a note and said she would get the message to her. A week or so later, I had another package for them, and the director was there. I had not taken any of my hour lunch break yet, so I took it while we chatted. I told her a brief version of my story and told her I was in the process of writing a book about my life. She said, "I really wish we had met a month earlier" because Auburn University had a keynote speaker at one of its social workers degree program events and that this lady wrote a book. She told me the title, and I told her that I was very busy with the kids, work, and getting ready for my deployment, but when I got to Afghanistan, I would have more time to getting around to reading it. She said, "You should" and went on about this foster kid who had a class action lawsuit against the state of Florida. Of course, with everything going on, that conversation and the title of the book were forgotten—forgotten until today! I told my roommate, Stettler, and he said, "That's somebody upstairs trying to tell you something, Hoss," and I was ecstatic, to say the least. This was *unbelievable*, and yet, once again, it really happened! God wanted me to read this book. His providence once again was revealed. Now, Ms. Ashley Rhodes-Courter, I will need not two as stated before, but three of those signed books from you. The last one will go to the lady director!

CHAPTER 17

Let Them Serve

As a foster kid and before I came into care, I obviously did not have a lot of possessions. At my real mom and dads' house, I don't even remember getting a single Christmas present or even knowing what Christmas was. One year for my birthday, I got a gray scooter and a bag of green plastic army soldiers. When I came into care, I remember filling out a wish list for Christmas that came from Agape. They would have an "adopt a foster kid wish list" that people could sign up for. Because of this, starting when we were teenagers up until Gabbi, Kentrell, and Elijah, Brittany and I would adopt a foster kid for Christmas through Agape. It was very important for my loving wife and me to pay it forward, and now that we are foster parents, it has been repaid to us—forward again. As it is written in the scriptures, you cannot outgive God (Malachi 3:10). Yes, we could afford to buy our foster kids presents, but it is very nice to be helped and to be served, and of course, we let them. Remember, it is not about you. It's the Lord's work. I say again, "Let them serve!"

CHAPTER 18

Bullies

As a foster kid going to school, I remember getting made fun of a lot. What I figured out as a young boy was that kids are cruel because they are ignorant or just plain mean. His name was James, and his questions were relentless, one right after another. He started with the clothes I was wearing and ended with my shoes. I distinctly remember him saying, "Can you not afford to buy shoes without holes in them?" I was thinking, *Man, I am just glad to have shoes on.* I had always had dirty old shoes; this was normal for me, but being that his parents had some money, and I think he was the only child, I guess he did not understand that there were kids his own age who were less fortunate than him. That might have been his or his parents' fault or, probably, a combination of the two. I must admit, very rarely do I let what people say affect me as I have attested in this book already, but because of him, I told my wife I would not fuss at her for buying my kids new shoes. They will not have holes in their shoes. This was a big deal for me as you will find out in my second book, *From the Foster Care Club to the Couple Comma Club(1,000,000): My Journey with God*, which I haven't written yet. My mother-in-law calls me frugal, but my wife calls me plain ole cheap!

CHAPTER 19

A Few Days in the Desert

Today it is June 14, 2014, in Afghanistan. I finished *Three Little Words*, and I had another jaw-dropping experience. Earlier in the book, she talked about a baby brother whom she had seen asleep in a wooden box. At the end of the book, she found out that her brother died of SIDS. Remember Michael, my little brother? Yes, the one who we were told died of crib death, also known as SIDS. *Wow*, this is *unbelievable*!

Yesterday (June 14th), Senior Airman Bennett asked me how I got to where I have when it comes to my finances. I told him about the seed that was planted, that I was cheap, and also about Dave Ramsey and his book *The Total Money Makeover*, a great book for financial peace. By the way, I strongly recommend it, and I did e-mail him while I was over here and asked if he would send me a signed copy of his book, and he did. How cool is that; thanks, Dave! I look forward to returning the favor with a signed copy of this book. I told Bennett I had the best ally one could have on my side when it comes to finances, and that was my God! I told him the prayer that I often pray—that is, if money would require my soul or my family, then not to bless me with it. But if I could continue to bless other people with it and give Him the glory, then, Lord, please continue to bless me as You have. Then I pray that I mean that prayer. You see, it is easy to say those words in the prayer, but it is really hard to mean it, and I pray that I do. In the Bible, it is stated, "For the love of money is a root of all *kinds of* evil, for which some have strayed from the faith in their greediness, and pierced themselves through with many sorrows. (1 Timothy 6:10). Did you hear me? Look it up yourself. I encourage you, too. It is the *love* of money that is the root of all evil, not money itself. The reason I bring this up is, today, I was talking to Brittany on FaceTime, and she said she could see us having four of our own kids—one biological and our three adopted ones—then, in about five to ten years, have all our real estate paid off, buy a bigger house, and start taking sibling groups of foster kids up to five at once! This would, of course, require her to quit her job and be a stay-at-home mom. I was really excited about this. As you already know, being a foster parent began as one of my dreams, and it came true, and now, it is one of hers! Of course, this would be very expensive, but I know the Lord knew that, and that is one of the reasons He has blessed Brittany and me like He has. I know He knows our hearts, and He is just answering those two prayers that I so often pray.

Today, June 16, 2014, is Father's Day back home. Brittany and the kids told me, "Happy Father's Day" over FaceTime, and I FaceTimed my dad to do the same. I feel like I don't communicate with my parents—especially, my dad—nearly as much as I should, but today we talked for a good while, and I enjoyed that. I thanked him again, face-to-face, for the sacrifices he and my mother made for my sister and me and asked him if it was worth it, and he said it was. After that, he asked if what he saw in the background was my dorm, or barracks, in Afghanistan. I showed him the empty room, which we turned into our hangout room, which was right next door to the one I was in, and showed him the shattered window—that was why it was empty—and I told him that a mortar round had caused it. The next question he asked was, "When did that happen?" I stated, "Oh, you know, it was years ago," then I said, "I'm lying to you right now." He got my message. Yesterday, in Afghanistan, I got an award for missing my first Father's Day, along with several other airmen.

As stated before, these are times you never get back. You only have your first Father's Day once, but even being deployed, it is worth it! What I guess I am really worried about is next year when I do my taxes; if, indeed, I get to adopt my three kids, then what will the IRS say? "Wow, this looks somewhat fishy. Mr. Oden went from zero to four dependents in an eighteen-month span." I guess I should tell my Certified Public Accountant to get ready for an audit.

CHAPTER 20

Count Your Blessings

Being a foster parent, you will find that you must think outside the box. Everything you know about a normal child, you may have to throw out. When we first got the kids, they would eat just about anything we put in front of them. When people would ask us if they were picky eaters, I would say, "No, I think they are happy just to have food." When we got Elijah, he would eat some of his food, then bring the rest to me, and ask me if I would save the rest so he would have something to eat later. I said, "Son, finish your food, and I promise, Daddy"—then I paused and added—"God and Daddy will make sure we have enough food to eat" (Matt. 6:26). This happened in front of one of my really good friends from church. He said, "You know, I have always taken for granted that I would always have enough food to eat, but seeing this really puts things into perspective for me." I told him, "Yes, foster kids and their stories, the sad, sometimes unbelievable stories will do that to you, it will definitely help you to remember the small things and help you count your blessings." What a blessing it was for us (Brittany and me) to be the ones to comfort our five-year-old Elijah, and when he prays, to hear him thank God for our food and each individual at the table by name. We know that he is, at least, starting to get it, get God! Praise God! When his Bible class teacher, who teaches the four and five-year-old Bible class, comes to us with tears in her eyes and tells us our son said the most beautiful prayer in class, we know he is starting to get it even more. In the Bible, we are commanded to preach and teach the gospel. Matthew 28:19–20 reads, Go "therefore[a] and make disciples of all the nations, baptizing them in the name of the Father and of the Son and of the Holy Spirit, teaching them to observe all things that I have commanded you; and lo, I am with you always, *even* to the end of the age." Amen." When I think of the great commission, I would always think of a missionary or teaching someone my own age about God, but I know this counts too, and to see him, along with his younger brother and sister, growing in the Lord—wow, yet another exhibit that makes it worth it. Even if they don't stay with us forever, I have no doubt that they will remember God, and that, for Brittany and me, gives us the passion we need to carry on!

The deployment (being that I wrote most of this book while deployed) is hard. Brittany did a few neat things for the kids and, I believe, for her as well before I left. First, she got the church youth group girls to fill a clear glass jar with about five hundred forty Hershey's Kisses. Each night, before they brush their teeth and after they say their prayers, they each get to eat just one, and she would tell them, "When the jar is empty, Daddy is coming home!" This was also when they would start talking about me—somewhat like therapy for the kids and Brittany. Next, she got the kids at church to make a construction-paper chain that had one hundred eighty or so links on it. They hung it around the perimeter of Gabbi and the boys' room. Each night, after eating their Hershey Kiss, they would take turns removing a link, and they knew that when all the links were gone, I was coming home. Lastly, we used the iPad to record me singing and rocking Gabbi to sleep to our song "Special to Me" by Martha's Trouble in my Air Force uniform. So each night my wife would rock her and play that recording for her, she would say, "Daddy" and kiss the iPad and sing it with me as I would rock and sing to my sweet little Great Gabsters to sleep. And they say you can't be in two places at once. Well, thanks to technology that the Lord has blessed us (military members) with, I can be over seven thousand five hundred miles away and still not miss a night of singing and rocking my little girl to sleep; praise God! For the most part, it worked, and Gabbi went right to sleep!

While writing this book, I got the idea of starting a foster care/ adoption foundation. I have decided to call it Richard Oden's Foster Care/Adoption Foundation. To me, and I think most would agree, who better to start a foster/adoption foundation than a man who was a foster kid, was adopted, then became a foster parent, and then, Lord willing, adopted his foster kids? I told you earlier that I had a calling—not only to complete my two life circles, but also I know the Lord is calling me to start this foster care/adoption foundation. I have been asked to speak a couple of different times about my life experience as a foster kid and a foster parent. I think the whole audience could agree on one thing. I am passionate about this work, and why wouldn't I be? As you can see, it has directly affected my whole life. My mission statement is as follows: to help as many foster/ adoptive kids and foster/adoptive parents face their Philistines and support them in any way we can. I pray that this work will be very productive and do exactly what my mission statement says and much more, and I know that with the Lord's hand and guidance, it will! I thank you for buying this book and would ask that you continue to support me and my efforts in this work by telling as many people as you can to do the same, and together, with God's hand, we can make a real difference!

Another Taliban Rocket Attack

Today, June 20, 2014, in Bagram, Afghanistan, we got indirect fire attack by three rockets. This is truly enough to make a man nervous, anxious, and old. However, whenever this happens, I always remind myself of two things: First is one of my favorite gospel songs,

"This World Is Not My Home." Second, I remember and claim Psalms 91—really, the whole chapter—but I will quote verses 11 and 12, "For he shall give his angels charge over you, to keep you in all your ways. In their hands they shall bear you up, lest you dash your foot against a stone." On Father's Day, while talking to my dad, I told him the reason I wanted to serve my country. As stated earlier, I wanted my flags. I went on to say I wanted a military funeral. He then said, "I don't want to be around to see it," and I truly believe, because of Psalms 91, he won't.

CHAPTER 21

Questions

When I tell people I was a foster kid, and then got adopted, the first question they ask me is, "Do you still know your biological parents?" The second question, like clockwork, is, "Have you tried to find them?" Third is, "What about your siblings and stepsiblings?" So I have to assume, you, my readers, would be asking these same questions as well. Therefore, I will be addressing these questions now. Well, like I said earlier, I haven't seen or heard from my biological father since he took off near my baby brother Michael's crib death. Really, my whole life up until recently, I had a big problem with the way he abandoned us. I used to dream about finding him. In that dream, when I found him, I grabbed him by the collar of the shirt and slammed him against the wall and said, "Did you not ever wonder how I turned out, I am your own flesh and blood! I can't imagine doing this to my kids! I am a good man, a productive member of society. I pay my taxes and serve my country! Did you not ever wonder?" When I got out of high school, I told Brittany and her dad that I wanted to find him. Brittany's dad said, "Richard, that may be a can of worms you don't want to be opened." I must admit, when he said that, I got a little upset, but the older and more mature I got, the more I realized he might be right and probably was. Slamming my father against the wall would only make me feel better in that moment. It wouldn't do any other good. I finally realized what to do about the feelings I had toward my biological father. I had to stop being a hypocrite! Remember, when one of my babies would say the phrase, "That's not fair," and I would immediately ask three questions: First is, "Are you in foster care?" Answer is, "Yes, Daddy." Second is, "Is that fair?" Answer is, "No, Daddy." Third is, "What do we do about that?" Answer is, "We get over it and move on." So that is my answer, and that's what I needed to do. What our dad did to us was not fair. It is not fair for any dad to do that to his children, and the only way I could get over it and move on was… well, this is the really hard part. Are you ready? I had to forgive him, and the older and more mature I got, especially in the Lord, the closer I got to doing exactly that. Also, it's like my three-year-old son tells his two-year-old sister, "You get what you get, and you don't pitch a fit."

As for my biological mom, I did speak to her sometime after I graduated college; she said, "Richard, I want to explain to you why I didn't get you kids back," but when she said this, I stopped her and said, " It doesn't matter now, don't tell me, I'm happy with the way my life turned out." As stated before, everything happens for a reason, but in my mind I was thinking that I did not want to give her the satisfaction of giving me an explanation. Once again, now that I am older and more mature in the Lord, I wish I would have let her talk. I don't think that if I did let her talk for her to say whatever, she would have told the truth. You see, my biological mom did have a lot of baggage. I do not know what all that baggage consisted of, but I can assume—and I do—that it wasn't at all good. The second half of what I told her was very true; I meant every word! I am really happy with the way my life turned out, and it did happen for a reason, but without her, because she chose not to abort me, I have this story to tell. Thanks, biological *mom*! That was the last time I talked to her; I was about twenty-one at that time, about eleven years ago. When I google both my biological mom and dad on the Internet, I do get to see a couple of pictures of them, but they are really rough looking; all are mug shots.

As for finding my biological parents now, I don't know; it might be like my father-in-law said—it might be a can of worms I don't want opened. Besides finding out my family's medical history, I don't know what good it would do, but if the Lord sees fit, then I will try to find them. I am not there yet, but as each day goes by, that is one day closer to being where I know I need to be—complete and total forgiveness. I am very close!

CHAPTER 22

A Divine Meeting

Today, June 22 in Bagram, Afghanistan, I met another foster parent. Every Sunday at 1300 we have a worship service at the chaplain's trailer. I did not know about this until last week, so today was my second service to attend. Lord willing, I will not miss another one as long as I'm here. Anyways, the chaplain takes prayer requests at the beginning. Once a request is made, he asks for another individual to pray for that specific request. I really like the way he has formatted this prayer, because the Bible tells us to bear one another's burdens in Galatians 6:2, and I quote, " Bear one another's burdens, and so fulfill the law of Christ." I feel like to pray for one another's requests is one way we can do exactly that. Today I requested prayers for this book. I told them I was a foster kid and now a foster parent, and the providence of God in my life was how this came to be. I asked prayers for this book to be used as a tool to bring glory not upon myself, but upon the Lord so that many people may come to know Him and know He is the one true living God. I also asked all the airmen to pray and ask God to bless this book so it could be simultaneously used as another tool for people to take that leap of faith with God and become foster/adoptive parents. After the service was over, an airman stopped me and said, "I am a foster parent in Alaska, thank you for your prayer request, it was the perfect time to hear that people are out there doing the same things we do." He was, of course, talking about us both being foster parents while being deployed. I was so excited to speak with him—men of faith, both deployed, and our wives back home. Being foster parents, we definitely had a lot to talk about. I asked him if he would mind if my wife called his just to check on her. He said that would be great and gave me his wife's phone number. When I told Brittany and asked her if she would mind calling, she said she didn't mind and she would. Later, I asked Brittany if she had called her yet, and she said, "Oh, I thought you meant, 'Call her someday,' not today." I told her I didn't do "somedays." The only someday I know for a fact will come is when the good Lord comes back again someday. The reason I thought I would write a book someday was, I thought of answering those questions above that were asked by people who found out I was a foster kid. I thought it would be neat if I could answer them in a form of a book, but of course, someday would never come for me. This simply was not enough motivation or reason for me to write this book; what actually got me to put pencil to paper was this: I looked at my life and saw the providence of God in my life and said I would be doing God a disservice if I did not share with other people how He has blessed me! I'm sure we have all heard it and probably even said it before; I know I have: "I'm going to exercise and lose weight someday. I'm going to stop smoking someday. I'm going to do better with my finances someday. I'm going to start my own business someday. I'm going to join the military someday. I'm going to write a book someday. I'm going to be a foster/adoptive parent someday." The problem with someday is that someday never comes. What does come is today or Monday through Friday plus Saturday and Sunday. She too got my message, and I respectfully hope you do too.

CHAPTER 23

My Hero

Today, June 22, 2014, is Brittany's birthday—back home. It is already June 23, 2014, here in Bagram, Afghanistan. If my math is correct, we are nine-and-a-half hours ahead of them back home. If you remember, on May 22, 2014, our tenth-year anniversary, I had a bright idea about getting her Edible Arrangements—fruit that looked like flowers, but you could eat it, thinking it would be for her and Annabelle, not to mention the other three kids, to enjoy. Well, I was right. She did like the thought behind it, but she said, "You know I like flowers." Redemption… how sweet it is. I did get her flowers with a balloon this time with a note that said, and I quote, "Hey, babe, you are so awesome, believe it or not, I do love you more than Gabbi Girl, barely, LOL. You are my hero, and you are doing so great. I am so proud of you and also so proud to be your husband, hbd 143 RO." She asked me what *hbd* meant, and I told her, "Happy birthday, crazy." She laughed and said, "Oh yeah, duh." The number 143 has been our code for many years. I think we started that seventeen years ago when we first started going out. It means "I love you," and it's a really good thing we had this, because the card only allowed two hundred fifty characters, and they included spaces as characters—that's just crazy—but I made it fit, and yes, I did use all two hundred fifty characters allowed. To all the military wives, husbands, families, and caregivers out there, like I told Brittany, you are heroes. You serve, too. The only difference is, you did not raise your right hand and volunteer to serve, but yet you go. You, too, take care of everything on the home front. You take on double the responsibility, playing Mom and Dad while simultaneously worrying about your loved one's safety. I often wonder, who has it harder—us or them?

On this very topic, a lot of people come and thank me for my service, I really appreciate that, but very few people stop and thank Brittany for hers. Think about this now, we just got three foster kids, my wife was pregnant, and we got informed that I was deploying to Afghanistan, so she had to take on my roll, take care of the kids, not to mention have our child while I was away. So time and again when I go to public speaking events the veterans will be asked to stand and get recognized, and I think that they should because I think that we have earned that, but they will stop there. I would ask them to go one step further and ask the veterans to sit and ask the families of the veterans to stand and get recognized. Because with three children, giving birth to our biological child, I think that Brittany has earned that. I think that there are many other military families who have definitely earned that as well! I actually did this at one of my public speaking events. Afterwards a lady came to me with tears in her eyes and told me that her husband had served in the Navy for over 22 years and not once has she ever been asked to stand and get recognized. She said it meant the world to her! Another of my dreams is to walk into a public speaking event after this book is released and hear the public speaker do exactly that. If this dream becomes reality I will know that God has used this as a tool to make my small mark on the world. Wow, what a blessing that would be!

As for my sibling and stepsiblings, I did get a chance to visit my older biological sister and a few of them while I was in high school. Brittany and I drove down to Fultondale, outside of Birmingham, Alabama. I had recently bought a truck before this trip, so when we pulled up, I got the feeling that they were thinking, "Rich kid—whoever adopted him had a lot of money and bought him this truck, and he was spoiled." I really can't explain it; that's just the vibe I got. "Lord, please forgive me if I am wrong." This, of course, was the complete opposite of the truth; my parents (the ones who adopted me) were great, but they did not give me a dime for any of my vehicles. I worked and saved and bought them myself. If this were the only thing, I would have gotten over it. However, Brittany felt very uncomfortable with the whole visit, to say the least, and I knew I was going to marry her. So I did what any good future husband would. I chose my future wife over pursuing a relationship with my sibling and stepsiblings. I just felt like a relationship with them would only lead to them asking us for money and putting Brittany and me into a lot of uncomfortable situations. Again, please, Lord, forgive me if I was wrong. So after we left that day, I decided I would no longer pursue a relationship with any of them; that did not mean, however, that they could not pursue a relationship with me. If I saw some effort from their side, I would be willing to reconsider, but in several years, I haven't seen any. Many young married people today can learn from the choice I made. You must choose your wife over your family. In my situation, it was an easy decision. In yours, it might not so much, but if you do what the scriptures say in Mark 10:7 and leave your father and mother and cleave to your wife, you will be blessed because this is the way God intended it.

CHAPTER 24

Make History

Make history; with my aircraft 88-0399 and me, I think we did just that. Little did I know my F-16 already had a history of its own. This particular fighter jet was, at one point, one of our former commanders of the 187th Fighter Wing. This commander went on to become a general who worked in the Pentagon. He was the general over the Air National Guard. While aircraft 88-0399 was my responsibility in Afghanistan, at one point, she dropped five out of ten bombs by our entire 187th wing—not to mention, helped save countless lives and helped the people of Afghanistan successfully have their first ever democratic elections. They told us about 60 percent of the population showed up to vote for their president, which is well over the average population we have to show for our presidential elections, and they risked their lives to do so. One day, Lord willing, I look forward to telling my children and grandchildren that I was part of what they read in their history books at school, something bigger than myself, and their mother and grandmother helped too each and every day by supporting me and taking care of things while I was away. I already told you that I got two bomb lanyards, and I gave them away, but I did not tell you what they represented to me, and those two that I gave away were my second and third ones given to me. I kept the first one given to me, and this is why: These lanyards on the bomb's job are to activate it when it is dropped. If the lanyard stays with the aircraft after the bomb is dropped, we know it is a live bomb and not a dud, but if it goes with the bomb, then we know it is a dud. My first bomb lanyard was handed to me by a pilot who dropped his first bomb in Afghanistan. I was told by another pilot later that "this is very rare and just does not happen," and the fact that he gave me his first drop was a big deal. At first, the pilot told me he wanted to give it to me, but since it was his first drop over here, he was going to keep it. Of course, I told him I understood, and then he started to walk away. When he got about ten paces, he turned around and said, "Oden, I have changed my mind, great job" and handed me my first bomb lanyard! Remember those flags—the ones I wanted so badly, the ones I wanted to earn by serving my country—well, those flags will be flown in my aircraft, 88-0399, in a combat sortie (mission) over Afghanistan while I am here. When I return home, I will get a shadow box for these flags, with my bomb lanyard displayed on the bottom. I will also get that pilot to sign that shadow box, and they will remain displayed somewhere in my house until the day I die, and those flags that flew in a combat zone over Afghanistan in my aircraft 88-0399 will be used. Well, you know what each one of them are for—the first to cover my coffin, the second to be folded up and handed to my wife or family, if she beats me to heaven, along with my bomb lanyard, and the third to fly over my gravestone. *What a moment in history that will be for our family!* I am humbled and honored I could be part of it! I would ask you now to do the same, not someday, but today! Remember, someday never comes, but you can make a commitment in your heart to make history today; be the first one in your family to become a foster/adoptive parent. I know everyone is not cut out for being that parent, but you can still make history by making a commitment to serve those who do take that leap of faith with God. Again, go the extra mile, get out of your comfort zone, and be passionate about this work and ministry! There are so many kids out there, and all the history they have is bad. You can be the one to turn their history around, and let me tell you, to be the family to do that—what a blessing! If you are a business owner, consider this: as a member of our military, I often receive military discounts, but not once have I seen foster care discounts. You could be the first business to offer such a thing, and I know, for people who are in the ministry and their supports, they will support you and your business and tell others to do the same. If you don't offer a military discount, consider doing that as well. You will probably get more business, and you can write it off on your taxes while simultaneously showing your support. Oh, by the way, all would apply to a foster/adoption parent discount as well—sounds like a win-win situation to me! There are so many things you can do to help our military and foster/adoptive kids and parents, and if you seek, you will find!

CHAPTER 25

The Fourth of July

Today, July 1, 2014, we were attacked again. I made my daily midnight walk to our building (my shift is from 0000 to 1200—midnight to noon for you nonmilitary out there), set my M16 rifle in its rack, and then proceeded to get a toolbox that we get every morning to work on our aircraft. The toolroom is beside a big bay door that we use to enter and exit the building with our toolboxes. When we are issued our toolbox, the standard procedure is to take full tool accountability for the tools in your box to make sure nothing is missing. The main reason we do this is to make sure there are not any tools left on the aircraft or the flight line that would cause foreign object damage, also known as FOD, and that was what I was doing just inside the open bay door when I heard it! *Buzz*, then someone yelled, "GET DOWN!" and I did, but the whole time I was looking in the air, what I saw was the phalanx exploding in the sky. This is a counter rocket weapon. Its job is to hit the rocket in midair and destroy it before it makes impact. It made sparkles in the sky like the Fourth of July, which was only a few days away. I was thinking to myself, *Man, I thought I was going to miss fireworks this year*. Not only did I not miss them, but they also came early. Then one of my buddies grabbed me by the backpack I was wearing and said, "Oden, get away from the door" the whole time dragging me across the floor away from the door. After it was over, I jokingly gave him a big hug and said, "My hero." I know, to some of you, this event would not seem funny at all, and to be honest, it is not funny to us either. It is in moments such as these, we are reminded of the bitter truth. There are people out there who hate us and want us dead. So, we deal with our stress the best way we know how—with humor and laughter. It's no secret that laughter is one of the best stress relievers. Many mental health professionals would agree, and let me tell you, if it works in these situations, it will work in just about any; try it. I strongly encourage you to laugh—yet another tool you can add to your arsenal!

Today I made a small world connection. I mistakenly tagged Lonnie Jones in a picture of myself on Facebook. I am really new at the whole Facebook thing, so I really did not know what I was doing. One of my buddies with whom I am deployed with asked me, "How do you know Lonnie Jones? I saw you tagged him in a picture on Facebook." I told him what I told you—that he was my youth minister and my counselor, not to mention a man I love, respect and look up to. He proceeded to tell me that Lonnie watched him grow up and that Lonnie and his father worked together at the Huntsville SWAT Team, where Lonnie was the chaplain, and I said, "Wow, what are the chances of us finding this out halfway across the world. It's a small one."

Today, it is the Fourth of July here in Bagram, Afghanistan. I FaceTimed with my wife while she was getting ready to eat dinner. She, the kids, and her parents were all at our house, grilling hamburgers with homemade french fries cut straight from the potatoes and put directly in the hot grease in the frying pan, with fresh ripe tomatoes—*yum*, one of my favorites—and on their Fourth, the next day, they were having grilled marinated chicken with baked potatoes (those are two out of three of my favorite meals back-to-back) with the Days and a more experienced couple from church, Brittany's parents, and my parents as guests. For a few minutes, I must admit, it got me somewhat down. I told one of my buddies, and he said,

"Remember, it's because of people like you that the Fourth of July is celebrated each year," and how true that was. I got over it. As stated before, I am honored to serve such a great country but more honored to serve such a great God! We, the citizens of this great country, need to not take for granted what we have here in the United States, how God has blessed us, and what it took to get us here. One other thing happened today that cheered me up; one of the pilots brought out a silly Uncle Sam pair of glasses that had the Uncle Sam hat and the mustache hanging down. We made a picture of two pilots holding the flag with me wearing the Uncle Sam glasses with some of the other members of cell two. Happy Fourth, everybody!

CHAPTER 26

Potential

Okay, I must address something that I said earlier in this book and correct it. At this time, this book has taken close to ten months for me to get from the beginning to here. It was true, but over that time frame, some things have changed. What I am talking about is when I made the statement that Kentrell showed the potential to be a really fun teenager—well, now that he has gotten comfortable and adjusted to the way he is supposed to act, he no longer shows that same potential. His older brother Elijah, on the other hand, has taken that potential and has run with it. Please don't misunderstand me. He is a really sweet, good kid, and we love him dearly. Our expectations for his behavior are high, as they should be, and recently, he has not met those expectations. Any other foster parent might cut him some slack and not insist that he behave like he should, but not me. I understand his situation more than most. I refuse to start letting his situation be used as a crutch. If I do that when he is five years old, he may never forget it and use it as a crutch for the rest of his life. I feel like some of my siblings have done this very thing and it is sad to see. I'm sure if you think hard enough, you too can think of people in your life who have done this, and if you have, I'm sure you agree—how sad, but don't be an enabler. I promise you, I won't. If I did give him some slack it wouldn't be because he was in foster care, but it might be because of my deployment. We know kids need their fathers, but sometimes, their father (mother and any military family

122

member) just can't be around and in situations such as a deployment, and this is a really good and justifiable reason. One day, Lord willing, we will get to adopt him and his younger brother and sister and they will all be old enough to understand why Daddy had to leave them for so long. So, we called DHR and got a referral to a licensed professional counselor. I don't know for a fact that this will help at such a young age, but it is another benefit of being a foster parent. It couldn't hurt to try. It certainly did help me.

CHAPTER 27

For a Reason

Today, July 6, 2014, is yet another Sunday. Man, this week flew by—praise God! That is one less week I have until my baby is born and one less week I have to wait to get to hold her, not to mention seeing Brittany and the kids. It won't be long now, only eight more paychecks. For the nonmilitary out there, all military personnel get paid twice a month—the first and fifteenth. The captain-chaplain said if I don't think about how fast the weeks are going by, they will continue to go by fast. Don't think about it… don't think about it… wait a minute. LOL. Today at church the captain gave a lesson from the Book of Joshua. At the end he said, "I don't know how God does it or why, but he takes our failures and somehow interweaves them together and makes something positive out of them." When he said this, I was thinking about my whole life in particular. I was thinking about our three miscarriages. Wow, he was exactly right. God does have the power to make anything and everything make sense if we just trust in Him! Also, today I asked the airman from Alaska, who is a foster parent as well, if he would write a piece for me to add in this book. I told him I wanted you, my readers, to have an unbiased point of view about being a foster parent, and who better than him, an airman I randomly met—correction—through yet another providence of God, I met in Bagram, Afghanistan. He said he would be honored. Although the pieces written by my past foster parents and adoptive parents are true and very helpful, I understand that they might be a little biased due to the fact they helped raise me, and I turned out okay. I think this airman and his wife might carry a little more weight because he just met me a couple of weeks ago. This is what they wrote:

As I was sitting in the Flightline Chapel one Sunday listening to the various prayer requests and praise reports throughout the church, one person's prayer request stood out among all the others I heard. I couldn't see who was praying as I just sat with my eyes closed focused on the prayers and praises. This individual's prayer request was that he asked us all to pray for his pregnant wife as she was carrying their little baby. However, they had some difficulties in the past. I continued to listen as this individual also requested that we pray for his foster children and their ability to adopt them. That Sunday, I went home and thought about my family and especially about my very own foster children especially two of them that had come up for adoption. My wife and I have four children of our own and an additional three foster kids currently in our care. I contemplated on the difficult situation that we were in, also, and on deciding whether or not to adopt the two that were up for adoption. My wife and I have had a very difficult time deciding as it is a huge undertaking just for foster care let alone to adopt these, at often times, very difficult but loving children. Another week had passed and I once again found myself sitting in the Flightline Chapel listening to the prayer requests when I

125

heard an individual speak up and ask for support as he is trying to write a book while he's
deployed about foster care. He went on to
explain how he too was a foster child and wanted
to write this book to encourage others to give it
a shot. It was at this point when I opened my
eyes to see who was talking. I pinpointed him
and went back to listening to the various others
prayer requests and praise reports. I continued
through the service, however, my heart kept
taking my mind to think about this individual
that had spoken about foster care. After church
was over, I stopped the individual and talked to
him, and he explained his story of going from
a foster child to becoming an airman in the
United States Air Force and also a foster parent
himself. I continued my chat with Richard, and
we found many things to talk about regarding
foster care. You see, I was having a very difficult
time deciding on whether or not my wife and I
should adopt our two foster children. After this
discussion, I knew that God Himself had placed
Richard's words in my heart at that moment for
a reason. Often we try to dismiss when God
puts His plan to work and shows us the sign,
only to complain later about not understanding
why we can't see something as a sign to push us
in a certain direction or help us make up our
minds. Was this my sign? Was this the answer to
my prayer of the need to understand what I was
supposed to do? I believe it was, and the more

I got talking to Richard, the more this became very evident.

You see I wasn't ever the person that wanted to do foster care; it was my wife's dream. She had spent years trying to talk me into it, and well, if you knew me a little bit, you would understand that I may be just a tee-ny-bit hard-headed. I finally gave into my wife's request under one condition: we were going to give this foster care thing a try, however, only one child at a time and absolutely no adoption. We attended training, as all foster parents are required to do, and took all the classes required by the state of Alaska. After all this was complete, we got our very first phone call asking us to take two children into our home. Remember, rule number 1, only one child. Well, I let this one slide with my wife's encouragement. We agreed to take these two kids and had child services bring the kids by, so we could meet them. These poor kids had gone through a horrific event, which we won't go into, and were in need of immediate placement. These wonderful kids were our first shot at foster care. This wasn't an easy thing. As you see, the little girl was very delayed developmentally wise, as was her older brother. Her older brother also suffered from FADS and was autistic. Wow, what had we gotten ourselves into we thought to one another. We had definitely bit off more than we thought we could chew. However, my wife once again ensured me that God will never give us more than we can handle, and that seemed to ease my anxiety quite a bit. Well, it eased my anxiety for the minute anyhow. As you may already know, many autistic kids have very loud outbursts that are very random and can be very hard to deal with. This boy's outbursts weren't screaming but instead giggling. This giggling could do nothing but make us smile (well, most of the time anyhow). Sometimes, these little giggling episodes happened at those very serious moments in church (you know when you aren't supposed to laugh) and at various other moments that were very serious to everyone around but definitely not him. He created a very special place in our hearts, and I can still hear his giggles when I think of him. We had these two children in our care for a year and a half and had an unbelievable time with them. These two kids, even with all their issues, didn't slow our life down in the terms of hobbies much at all. We gained so much insight to what truly mattered. Granted, we lost some sleep, but we were gaining so much more. I learned so much about these kids, my own children, and definitely what my wife and I could handle as a team. The day came very sudden when we received a phone call telling us that child services would be at the house the next day to pick these kids up as they were going back with their mom. This was a very difficult moment because we had been told the entire time that she wasn't even close to being ready to get her children back. We had to let these two kids go, out of our care, and it became a very sad day for my entire family. You see, I saw what my own kids did for these two foster children, some unbelievable things, and it amazed me daily. My very own kids were doing exactly as kids do and loving unconditionally. They were teaching us Jesus's message of love. They didn't know what these kids had been through, and it didn't matter. All they knew is that they had a new brother and a new sister, both whom they had come to absolutely adore. Adore so much that I watched my very own little girl learn how to truly open up her heart and show her love. See my daughter is a very shy little girl who has the absolute sweetest heart, but she keeps her external emotions very controlled. I watched my three-year-old son act like he was a big brother to the seven-year-old boy and try to help him wherever he could. I watched my six-year-old boy treat him like he was his best friend and always gave him a hug to let him know he was loved. I watched my oldest boy, who was eleven, open his heart and his room to this boy and learn to appreciate all those special giggles and cooing he would do for hours as he tried to calm himself to sleep. When I watched the vehicle pull off with our first two foster kids and watched as my family wept like we were having our own kids taken from us, it tore me up. It felt like someone was taking two people from our family—wait a minute, they were. It was very hard, but we had to accept that the mom needed another chance. We currently stay in contact with the mom and have gotten to have the kids come over to visit and stay with us. We can notice changes, but one thing that makes our hearts happy is knowing that they have a home.

Remember how I told you God works in amazing ways. Well, this incident was no different. It was that very night that we received a phone call to take in a different foster child back into our care. We had already had him for a short term, and they were needing a home for him as his mother had once again had a relapse. This particular child was also autistic, and he was very difficult to handle. I don't think we would have been able to take him back on if we still had the other two. It wasn't long after, when my wife called and said she had agreed to take on two more foster kids. Did you catch what I said about my wife calling me? Did I mention that this was while my brother-in-law and some of our kids and I were on a fishing trip? "Are you serious?" I asked her on the phone. I mentioned that most worry about things when they go away. However, I didn't think I had to worry that I would come home to a couple extra kids. As I talked to my wife a little more, I agreed we would talk about it more when I got home. I put the phone down, turned to my brother-in-law, and said, "Well, I guess we have a couple more kids at the house." He just laughed, though I didn't think it was nearly as funny. As we pulled into the driveway, my wife caught me at the camper and said she also failed to mention that these kids had lice. Now, that really topped it off. I already wasn't sure I wanted these kids but I knew I definitely didn't want the bugs. I got over it pretty quickly as I walked in the door and was confronted with these two kids that went right to saying hi to me like they had known me forever. Time went on, and these two became part of the family very quickly, however, not without many stressful days.

As for the three-year old that was in our care, he was getting better. His mother is still trying, and we hope that he will be able to reunite once again with his mother as she has had some difficulties in life but never a difficulty of showing and giving her love to her son. I pray that she can find her way and once again get her child back. However, for now, we will just continue to enjoy every moment and outbursts he provides us in the time being. Now back to the other two kids. You see these children lacked the structure, but more importantly, their whole life they were missing out on the love and affection that they so desperately needed. They needed as much as you could possibly give them. Sounds easy, does it not? Just love them back, you're thinking. Well, I thought that as well until I soon realized I couldn't give them enough. They needed constant affection and would come in between me and any other kid that might be talking to me at the moment or wrestling around with me. I learned that this was a phase; however, it was still very difficult. It has gotten much better but is still very trying at times. These two were learning our structure and household rules however some of my kids were struggling to let them fit in, as were my wife and I. We knew we loved them to pieces but weren't sure we could continue to deal with so much and put our other kids through it. We struggled with the understanding and talked about it daily. We knew our children would follow our lead and would accept them as their own flesh and blood. That was when we did the same.

I left for Bagram, Afghanistan, and had a big decision to make. Would we adopt these two children that had been to nine different homes in their short five years for the boy and six years for the girl? It seemed like a question that I just couldn't bring myself to answer at the moment. I loved them so very much. However, I still thought of just continuing to foster without adopting and letting these two go to a different home. You see, the devil was tempting me to take the easy road. He was there to whisper in my ear that we would be better off to just let them go back into foster care and hope that they get adopted. I had been struggling with this decision, although knowing what decision God ultimately wanted me to make. When I heard Richard speak up and praise his foster parents for the life they allowed him to have, I knew that God had placed him in that chapel, on that very day, for a reason. The reason was so His words through Richard could resonate within my heart and make me understand the path that God was providing me with. You see, that is the great thing about God. He will provide us a path, and we can chose to take it or not. He allows us the free will to make the decision. When we make the wrong one, He is there to once again provide a path for us. What an amazing God we serve! I had made up my mind at that very moment and later called my wife and could hardly tell her the news quick enough. I let her know that I was going to listen to God and heed from His sign He provided through Richard and his words that day. We are currently going through the steps to adopt, but it will have to continue when I get home. I continue to see Richard at church each Sunday, and we stay after just talking about life. We obviously talk about his life of being a foster kid as well as talk about the lives of both of us as foster parents. I would have never thought that I would be the one to be a foster parent, let alone one that adopts more children when we already had four kids of our own. Nor, did I think that God would provide the answer to my prayer while deployed to Bagram, Afghanistan. I believe in the work God does and believe wholeheartedly that He chose to put Richard in that church that day so his words could be spoken. Thanks be to God for providing everlasting direction to me and my family. Thank You for blessing me with the ability to open my heart and do Your work for these children. Thank you for allowing Richard's words to light a fire in my heart and invigorate me to take the difficult step. I know this won't be an easy path. However I know, without a doubt, that I can give these children a life they can look back on and appreciate. I know I can provide these children with the ability to speak humbly to God and thank Him for what He has provided. I know I can give these children the love that God wants each one of us to give and receive. I know I can give these children a mom and a dad, a mom and dad that love them and will be there for them when they have a difficult day. I know that I can give these children a chance at life just like Richard received. Thanks, Richard, for listening to God and providing me with the much needed words that day. Not only am I thankful, but my two foster kids are thankful as well!

Sgt Nick Weiers

This is awesome. My wife and I both had tears while reading it and afterwards. We do, indeed, serve a great God! And he has blessed both of us by bringing us together halfway across the world—in Bagram, Afghanistan, of all places. Thank you so much. One of my many goals for this book has already come to fruition through you both, and it's not even finished yet. Praise God! Thanks again for your caring and loving hearts; for being there for those kids when no one else was; and more importantly for showing those kid the love of God.

In the Bible, Matthew 25:34–40 reads, "Then the King will say to those on His right hand, 'Come, you blessed of My Father, inherit the kingdom prepared for you from the foundation of the world: for I was hungry and you gave Me food; I was thirsty and you gave Me drink; I was a stranger and you took Me in; I was naked and you clothed Me; I was sick and you visited Me; I was in prison and you came to Me.' "Then the righteous will answer Him, saying, 'Lord, when did we see You hungry and feed You, or thirsty and give You drink? When did we see You a stranger and take You in, or naked and clothe You? Or when did we see You sick, or in prison, and come to You?' And the King will answer and say to them, 'Assuredly, I say to you, inasmuch as you did it to one of the least of these My brethren, you did it to Me."

I now fully understand what Jesus meant when He said that, and that is thanks to you and any and all foster/adoptive parents. So, my brother in arms and in Christ, I know there is truly a special place in heaven for people like you both. God bless! PS—Brittany and I both have always wanted to visit Alaska. God works in mysterious ways, wouldn't you say! LOL!

CHAPTER 28

A Few More Days in the Desert

Today, July 8, 2014, we got attacked again by three rockets, but this time it was different from all the rest. This time, the Taliban attacked during daylight hours, which hasn't happened since I have been here. It also doesn't make any sense because this is right in the middle of their Ramadan, a religious holiday for Muslims, when they can't eat, fight, or work all day. I was sitting at one of the computers inside the building when I heard, "Get down," and of course, we all did. We again heard the phalanx, but this time we heard and felt the explosion. It's like something you would see in a movie, but it's real life. I thank God that my family and my fellow Americans back home don't have this imminent threat back in the States. I would gladly serve on many other tours to make sure they never have this kind of threat. I do realize that other countries aren't so lucky, like Israel—yet another reason to be thankful you are an American.

Yesterday, July 13, 2014, was one of the worst days since I've been here. We are closing in on the midway point of this deployment, and I guess this is when the fatigue—or whatever they call all the emotions one is having while deployed and missing their loved ones, not to mention all the other things that are going on here—starts to get to you. Thank the good Lord that today was Sunday, and I got to go to worship service; that really helps. I also went to talk to a senior master sergeant who was a first shirt, not ours, but another unit's. She was teaching a class on public speaking, for which I signed up to take. I wanted to attend her class that was scheduled for 1:00 p.m., but that was the same time our worship service started. So I called and asked her if I could come to the later class that started at 8:00 p.m., and she said that was fine. Unfortunately—or just maybe fortunately—I slept late and got there about thirty minutes late to discover that the class was cancelled because nobody showed up. I asked the airman who told me this; if the first shirt, SMSGT Weatherspoon, was in her office so maybe I could go over the material in the class that she was teaching. He pointed me in the direction of her office, and I went. To my surprise, she was there. I told her who I was and why I was there, and she said, "Come on in and take a seat, and we can go over the class together." Well, to make a long story short, the material in the class—which, on a normal basis, would have taken about twenty minutes or so to go over one-on-one—took about three hours, but of course, we talked or, should I say, I did most of the talking, and she listened. I was having a rough day and she may never know how much she helped me out that day. She is a really young lady for all the stripes (her rank) that she has, and she is active duty, and that says a lot about her. We talked some about public speaking and a lot about this book and my kids. Because she was an African-American, I asked her if she thought my kids would one day have a problem with us being white, and if so, how she would handle it. She went on to tell me that her kids had a white grandfather, and to her kids, that was just their granddad. That comforted me, and I pray that if that does, in fact, become a problem, I will remember times like these in the present when all I am thinking and praying about is for God to let me adopt these babies.

Today, July 14, 2014, when I FaceTimed with Brittany and the kids, I told her that whenever I see my three-year-old Gabbi, I think about how I so badly want to be the one to walk her down the aisle on her wedding day and that when I think about that, I start to tear up. She then said, "What about me?" and I told her, "You got this, woman," and I told her how awesome it was for me to sit back and watch her work. She then said, "Daddies are supposed to be there for their firstborn children, I'm just throwing that out there." She was just picking on me, so I responded with, "You get what you get, and you don't pitch a fit!"

Today, July 21, 2014, it got real. As usual the rocket-attack sirens went off, and we all got down, but this time we could hear the rockets whistling in. When it landed, some could hear it bounce off the flight line and obviously feel the vibrations of the impact. It was the first time since I have been here that I cringed when a rocket landed. One of my buddies said, after he saw me cringe, I turned pale. I shook it off and was okay for the moment, but when we got the all clear and got to go see the impact marks, it shook me up again. You see, a piece of one of the rockets made impact on spot 18, about fifteen feet from the crew chief's toolbox. The crew chief was usually walking around his aircraft and/or standing at his toolbox, doing his paperwork, a.k.a. forms, for his aircraft. There was a metal bomb stand sitting against the wall the projectile hit; it sliced through it like a hot knife goes through butter, pierced the wall barricade, and came to a stop two taxiways over. Out of all the places it could have hit on the whole entire base, it hit here. Luckily, the crew chief assigned to this spot was inside. By the way, the aircraft in this spot was aircraft 88-0399. Two more rockets hit our area this day; one went through the fuel barn, and the other went through the phase dock barn. The latter one hit where some of our airmen were working, but it did not detonate the explosives inside. This day could have been a lot worse than it was. Before I left for Afghanistan, my family and I were invited to eat dinner with the Bear family from church. After a great time of fellowship, we had a scripture reading and a prayer session. Before the prayer session, I asked if we all could get down on our knees and talk to God, and we did. The purpose of that prayer session was to ask God to protect me and all the men and women I would be serving with. After I saw the impact and where it was, I asked to go speak to the chaplain. It was after thanking God in prayer with the chaplain and talking about the events of that morning when I remembered that prayer session with the Bears. Earlier in this paragraph, I used the word *luckily*. I would like to take that back and say two main reasons the crew chief assigned to spot 18 was not outside, and no one else got injured or killed today: first, again, Psalms 98, and this was just one more prayer answered from our one true living God! I have caught some flak from some of my fellow crew chiefs for wanting to go talk to the chaplain. However, in my humble opinion, it takes more of a man to ask for help than it does just to hide it and take it out on the people whom they love the most. You see, we can't talk about what goes on over here to our loved ones back home for fear of worrying them. Remember, I am an advocate for counselors because they have helped me and I do practice what I preach.

Today, July 28, 2014, my wife is really starting to show but it really hasn't hit me yet—being a biological father—but as each day goes by, it is certainly starting to. I hope Annabelle likes me when I finally get to hold her because just like our heavenly Father, I already *love* her, and she is not even born yet!

Today, July 29, 2014, Brittany sent me this message:

> I miss you! Even though you are missing Annabelle's birth, I'm really glad you joined the Air Force. Your time at basic and now deployed always makes me appreciate you and love you more! I hope with the chaos of four kids, we won't take the each other for granted or forget we loved each other first. I'm glad we found each other so early in life and are still in love

seventeen years later. I love you and I am glad
to get to grow old with you. You are my favorite!

Remember when I discussed Brittany's father and his decision
to send her away to college? It was while in basic training for the Air
Force and this deployment that I was finally able to let go of being
upset at him. Again, God knew this was in our future, and he used
her going out of town to college as a tool to prepare us for this.

Today is September 11, 2014, in Afghanistan, where I am. My
baby, Annabelle Elizabeth Oden, was born on September 10, 2014,
back home in Alabama, and she weighed eight pounds and six ounces
and was twenty-one and a half inches long. Both she and Brittany
are doing great; praise God. I can't describe to you all the emotions
I had when she was born, but I can sure try. Although I haven't even
officially met her yet, I already love her so much. I keep thinking
of my father and many fathers like him who don't even know their
own children. I didn't get that before kids, and certainly don't get
that now. I also think about my foster children and myself when I
was a foster child. My parents did such an honest and good job not
treating me any different than their biological children. I mean, yes,
I did get in trouble a lot, but never once did I feel like I was treated
any different than my brothers and sisters, their biological children.
In fact, I remember one conversation when we were talking about
twins and how it ran in both my family and Brittany's family. My
adoptive mom had my identical twin sisters, and my wife's mom is
a twin. When my mom heard this, she said, "Oh, oh, Richard and
Brittany, you could have twins too!" Of course, I had to pop her
bubble when I had to remind her that genetics wouldn't play a role
on my side because she adopted me. It was pretty neat that she forgot
she did so. So, I will make the same commitment to my foster and,
hopefully, adoptive children.

CHAPTER 29

Fill You In

It has been one year and five months—that is, seventeen months, or about five hundred fifteen days, since my last entry in this book when my daughter Annabelle was born, and I was still in Afghanistan, and a lot—I mean a lot—has happened since that great day. I will try to fill you in the best I can. Hang on; this will be lots of fun!

It is February 20, 2016, and once again I find myself in Montgomery, Alabama, on drill weekend. I am currently in a hotel in Hope Hull, Alabama, on a Saturday night after my drill with the 187th Fighter Wing, contemplating on where I should begin. I guess I will start right where I left off, and that is Annabelle's birthday.

So it was September 9 in the States and, of course, September 10 in Afghanistan, where I was. I got a call from Brittany saying that she wasn't feeling well, and she thought it was a case of Braxton-Hicks. I remember her saying, "If this is Braxton-Hicks and not real labor, this is so cruel." I told her not to chance it and go ahead and call Becky, her best friend, to get the ball rolling on everything they planned when Annabelle decided she was coming, and she did. It turned out that it was Annabelle and not a case of Braxton-Hicks. So they FaceTimed me when they got to the hospital, but nothing was happening except your normal "hurry up and wait," dilation, what the doctors said, etc. So because I just got off a twelve-hour shift, Brittany told me to try to get some sleep, and she would have Becky call me if there were any more developments. I can't say I got much sleep because of the anticipation, but I might have gotten a few minutes of rest. The next day, September 10 in the States and September 11 in Afghanistan, where I was, was when I got the FaceTime call! I was in my dorm room–like a room with a bunch of my buddies who had just gotten off work—you talk about a unique experience. I was on the phone on FaceTime in my bottom bunk with a cover draped over the top bunk so I could have some privacy while a few of my closest buddies were there in support of me and my family while she was being born! I'll never forget that! Leading up to the actual delivery, I had a reality moment; it was, indeed, September 11, 2014, where I was in Afghanistan, and we were told to be on high alert for indirect fire simply because of that date. By the time I realized this, Brittany's dad and family had made it to the hospital, so I asked him to step out of the room so I could tell him this. I said, "I really don't know how to tell Brittany this right in the middle of labor, but it is September 11, and there is a good chance she may hear a bunch of commotion—us hitting the deck and explosions. Can you tell her?" I guess I should have been a little bit more specific; what I wanted him to do was break it to her nice and easy, but that's not exactly how she was told the news. He marched right up to her and said, "Brittany, you need to prepare yourself, it is September 11 over there, and you might hear some explosions if they get attacked." Thanks, Pops, I could have told her that. LOL! As I said, Annabelle was born, and all things were good for a while, but on her sixth day she started getting jaundice really badly. Her level was 27.4. I knew it was serious when Brittany called me, crying, and told me that they would have to rush her on a baby ambulance called the Angel One to the NICU in Baptist South Hospital in Montgomery, Alabama, because this hospital could handle her situation. After getting this news, I felt completely helpless. What was jaundice? Was it as bad as it seemed to be? So, I had an NCO (noncommissioned officer) who had a wife who worked in labor and delivery. I told him the situation and asked him to ask his wife and to give it to me straight, and he did. His wife told him that at the levels she had, it was a possible brain damage scenario if they did not get that number down fast. With this news, I told my superiors, and they contacted the Red Cross to get me home early on emergency leave.

Now, let me say this: it was both the US Air Force and the Red Cross that got me home early on emergency leave, and I am very thankful for both on that decision. But if it were just me, my wife, and Annabelle, more than likely, I wouldn't have gotten to come home early. But because we still had three foster kids in Opelika, and they couldn't just stay with anybody (they had to stay with a licensed foster home), and Brittany had to be in Montgomery to feed Annabelle and, of course, be there for her, the Red Cross determined that this was, in fact, a hardship, and I got home about a month early! This was bittersweet for me. I had already accepted the fact that I was not going to be there for my baby's birth and had spent five months with my brothers- and sisters-in-arms and was really looking forward to us all coming home together, but as it should be, my family came first.

It took about four days for me to get from Bagram Airfield, Afghanistan, to Montgomery Regional Airport, and the whole time, Annabelle was still in intensive care but was improving every day. I arrived in Montgomery on September 18. It was great to see my wife and in-laws at the airport, but obviously, I could not wait to hold my baby for the first time! The good thing was, Annabelle was already in a Montgomery hospital, the city I flew into; the bad part was, because she was still in intensive care, they had specific visiting hours, and it was about an hour-and-a-half wait before I could see her. So we went to the hotel, and I nervously waited and chatted with some friends of mine who came with Brittany to see me home. When the time finally arrived, I was really nervous. It is really hard to explain why I would be nervous meeting my own daughter for the first time. I guess, because maybe not seeing her or holding her in real life made it somewhat like a story. But once I met her and held her, there was no denying that I was one of two people responsible for such a sweet, innocent little thing, and I think it had something to do with my father and what he did to us. The first time I held her when she was eight days old, I knew I was not like him, and oh, by the way, she proved to me in her own way she was mine, because right when I picked her up, she filled her diaper up! I imagined her saying, "Well, Daddy, that's what you get for missing my birthday!" LOL! I have pictures of that day on my website, www.fulllifecirclesquared. com. That same night, Annabelle was discharged from the hospital, but because Brittany and I both had a long day, we stayed in the motel in Montgomery and decided to go home to Opelika, Alabama, the next morning. The other kids did not know I was home, so I decided to surprise Elijah at his school and Gabbi and Kentrell at their day care the next day. That night at the hotel, Annabelle was real fussy, so I walked her throughout the hotel so my beautiful wife could sleep. I guess I figured she had paid her dues, dealing with all this by herself, without me there, and the least I could do was let her sleep, and not to mention, I was still suffering from jet lag and could not sleep anyway.

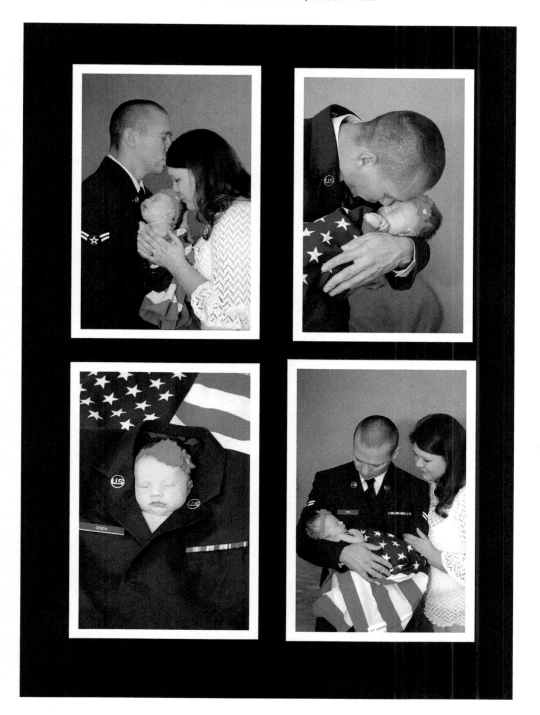

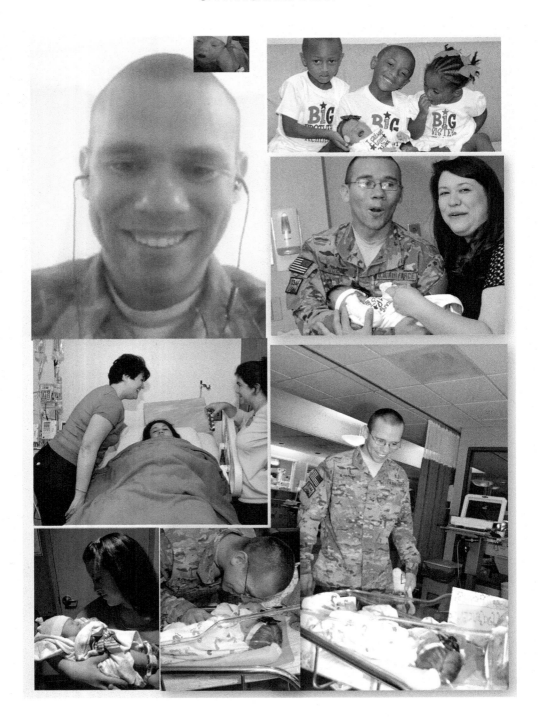

CHAPTER 30

That Guy

The next day was a Friday. I called the news and the paper and asked them if they would be interested in doing a story of me surprising my foster kids because I got back from Afghanistan early, and of course they did. That experience was awesome. I also knew that if the media would cover this story, I could use it as an opportunity to tell the rest of my story and encourage more people to become foster/adoptive parents. I'm sure you have all seen the videos of military surprising their families, the ones that will make you cry. I never thought in a million years that I would ever get to be that guy. Well, let me tell you, it is all it is cracked up to be to see the surprise and excitement on their faces. I would almost deploy again voluntarily—key word there being *almost*, of course! This video link is also on my website. Let me encourage you, if you get a second, please watch and make sure you have some tissues nearby!

The following Monday, DHR called and verbally reprimanded us for showing our foster kids' faces on TV. Apparently, that was a big *no-no*! But it was great publicity for getting DHR some more foster parents, which there is always a need. Keep in mind that DHR was the least of my concerns at this point in my life. I had just gotten out of a combat zone on emergency leave because my baby was in ICU, and of course, I missed my wife and other children as well.

CHAPTER 31

Back to Civilian Life

After I had readjusted to civilian life, things got back to somewhat normal—if you can have a somewhat normal life with four kids. We went to visit family in Huntsville, Alabama, and I only took a week off at UPS. I really just wanted to get my civilian life started back again. I do remember, the first Wednesday I was back at work at the Village Mall in Auburn, they tested the tornado sirens. The city of Auburn would always test them like clockwork—every Wednesday at twelve o'clock. Well, after being deployed, I forgot about this. I was walking down the mall, pulling my dolly full of packages, when I heard it. Can you guess what it sounded just like? Yep, it sounded like the sirens we heard in Afghanistan to let us know to hit the deck and take cover because the rockets were shot and on their way! So, I know some people saw me. I hit the floor, taking cover behind my stack of boxes. I didn't stay there but a couple of seconds, and some guy said, "Hey, buddy, you okay? You seem a little jumpy." I just told him yes and went on delivering my UPS packages.

CHAPTER 32

The Children's Trial

Soon after my return home, the case on my three foster children had finally come to trial for TPR, or termination of parental rights. Just to make it to trial was a big feat, but if we could get over this hurdle and get TPR granted, we felt like we could somewhat start to breathe easier, and our kids would most likely stay with us, and we would, of course, adopt them. There were many attorneys involved and I was asked to testify in front of the family court judge in Opelika along with my wife. The trial was set. I took off work that day. We sat outside the courtroom for about five hours or so and finally were asked to come in. To our dismay, the judge said that at first their biological mom was going to represent herself but, at the last minute, changed her mind, and so this proceeding had to be postponed so that her attorney would have some time to prepare. The judge was not at all happy with, what I would call, this stall tactic, but of course, these were not his words; they were mine. There was one more thing that we found out that day that really started to bother us. Gabbi was her brothers' sister by their biological mom, but she had a different dad. Well, apparently, her biological dad asked one of Gabbi's aunts to try to get her, and so she agreed that she would try to get custody of Gabbi.

We started to worry; surely, the judge wouldn't split Gabbi from her two brothers or take her away from us. This would devastate her, not to mention us, but again, it takes special people to be foster parents, and we knew anything could happen. At church, I asked the congregation to please pray that this would not happen, but if it did, pray that we would be comforted by His word and His people. I asked them to pray so hard and often, to bombard God with prayer so that God would be like, "Wow, another prayer for the Oden family, I guess I'd better work this out for them. I'm really tired of hearing about it." I know it really doesn't work like that. I was, of course, being facetious, but I hope you all got my point. I think the congregation did!

The next trial date was set. Again, I took off work and was pretty nervous. One thing it did do was to give us a little more time to think about what we were going to say when we testified in front of the judge. I told Brittany, "Okay, babe, this is the real thing, don't get nervous and raise the wrong hand when you affirm in." You will never guess who did exactly that when it was his turn to testify—yep, yours truly! Wow, that was really embarrassing! I told the judge that I really hurt for these children because I knew what they had been through. I had been in their shoes. I told him, Brittany and I would adopt these children if TPR was granted. I also told him we taught them who God was and what love was. One more thing, I also testified to the judge words that came out of his own mouth but were true. A week or so before, he (the judge) was being interviewed on the radio, and he talked about how important it was for all children's parents to build character in their children, so I told him that we thought these children needed parents who would build character in them and that Brittany and I were doing that and it would be a shame if we could not continue to do so. I think he realized where I got that from because although I was the only one in the courtroom to catch it, he did give a huh and a little smirk. It was neat for me to testify for my case in keeping these children, using his own words! I was asked by Gabbi's biological father's attorney, if we got to adopt her, would we allow her to have contact with him? I explained to the court how Brittany and I were different foster/adoptive parents. But, because of my background and if my adoptive parents had kept me from seeing my biological parents, then I would have been very upset with them. This was something they never had to deal with because my biological parents were nowhere to be found. So yes, as long as we felt like there was no harm in the relationship, we would allow him to see Gabbi if we got to adopt her. Although I did not tell the court or their biological mother and Gabbi's biological father, who were both in the courtroom that day, I was thinking and have told Brittany many times before, if they did maintain contact, those very hard questions I knew would be coming from my children—some of the very hard questions I, in fact, ask myself. I, as (hopefully) their adoptive dad, would not have to try and answer. I could say, "Hey, why don't you ask them yourself." One last thing that happened that day in the courtroom was, Gabbi's biological father got a chance to hear some of my story, that I was a foster kid, and so was he, and he asked his attorney if he could shake my hand before I left the court-room, and that's what happened.

The next few weeks were the longest weeks for Brittany and me. We had to wait for the judge's decision. Every time my phone would ring, I would rush to answer it, hoping it would be our attorneys telling us some good news. Would the judge not grant TPR at all? Surely, he wouldn't do that. This had been going on for about two and a half years now. Would he just grant TPR for the boys, Elijah and Kentrell, and not for their sister, Gabbi, who had a different father? That last one worried us the most. It took about two weeks, but we finally got the answer, and it was TPR granted for all three siblings. Praise God and hallelujah!

CHAPTER 33

Hurdles

So now all the major hurdles were crossed, and we thought it would be a short time between TPR being granted and us getting to adopt our children. Boy, were we wrong. Both their biological mom and Gabbi's biological father appealed the judge's decision of TPR. Brittany and I started doing research on how many appeals got overturned when TPR was granted. Thankfully, we found out that this almost never happened. I think they were using this right as a stall tactic, but for me, I was thinking, *Well, this is somewhat annoying because they're just delaying the inevitable.* But if contact between our children and their biological mom or Gabbi's biological father did come to an end (which I think for him it will) and the question came to me, I could honestly tell my children, "Your biologicals did everything that the courts would allow them to do to get you back."

Today, March 9, 2016, a Wednesday, and I am at home. Me at home on a workday, this hardly ever happens. I can probably count on one hand the number of times I called into work sick at UPS, and I will have been there for fifteen years on June 6 of this year. There is only one thing I can think of that would cause me to do so; that would be the dreaded stomach bug. This is the second day in a row I had to call into work. Annabelle got it first and was kind enough to give it to her daddy. When she got it a few days before, Brittany was frantically barking out instruction so the rest of the family would not get it. She said, "Put this vapor rub on your stomach and your feet, I know it may be a wives' tale, but it can't hurt." I said, "That's dumb, I'm not doing that," and guess who was the only one to get it? Yeah, I guess I like to learn the hard way. I did tell her, the next time, if I were the only one to get it, then I would do anything she told me. If she said, "Put your right leg behind your head and walk around the house like a crab," wives' tale or not, I was doing it. I have gone to the doctor and am feeling a lot better, so now I wanted to take advantage of this time off to work on the beginning of the end of this book. My publisher said the deadline for the rough draft is at the end of the month so it would be ready to be released on Veterans Day.

We got over one of the last of our hurdles by TPR being granted. At this point, we started having monthly visits with an adoption worker from DHR. We were excited but at the same time knew anything could happen. It was at these monthly meetings we got to start learning about our foster children's past. We got about a four-inch thick mound of paperwork for each (that is a foot thick of paperwork combined) of our three children. What we got to read was so tragic. I really don't want to go into much detail about it in fear that our children might read this book, and Brittany and I want to be the ones to decide how and when to tell them. I will say, one of the saddest things we read was that when Gabbi was just a toddler, the records stated that her Mama's boyfriend would pick her up by her hair. It was at this meeting we finally came up with the date for the adoption.

CHAPTER 34

Adoption Day

The day finally came, January 29, 2016, adoption day. I called the news and asked if they were still interested in the follow-up story they said they would like to do if we did, indeed, get to adopt our children. Of course, they said yes. I knew that this was yet another opportunity to encourage others about fostering and adoption and encouraging our military. Again if you have time, please go to my website to view a few of these articles! Please take the time to read each. They did a great job, and I don't think you will be disappointed.

After the adoption ceremony, we all went to lunch. It was great to have our first official meal together as Odens. That day I completed my second circle in my full life circle squared. I went from being adopted out of foster care on May 15, 1994, to adopting our children out of foster care on January 29, 2016! One thing I did not get quoted on in the articles was the way I felt after the adoption papers were finally signed. All I could think about was that sigh of relief I took when I got about one thousand or so feet above the war-torn country of Afghanistan on my way home. During the deployment, you try not to let yourself think about what could have happened. Although it's not exactly the same sigh of relief, the one I took in the courtroom that day was very similar. My mom got quite emotional and said that this was an answered prayer that she had been praying since she adopted my sister and me twenty-three years ago. I asked her to write it all down, and she did. This is what she sent me via e-mail:

Hi Richard!

I'm sorry it has taken me so long to sit down at the computer and send this to you! I just wanted to explain to you why I was so emotional at the courthouse during the adoption proceedings.

First, it was an emotional event because it reminded me of the day that we adopted you and Laura! It brought back a flood of memories from that day in May (May 15, to be exact) when we finalized the adoptions of the two of you in Judge Riddick's courtroom at the Madison County Courthouse.

Second, I was emotional because I was touched at the difference this was going to make in the lives of Gabbi, Kentrell, and Elijah! And, Dad and I were just so proud of you and Brittany for adopting the three siblings, whom we had grown to love as our precious grandchildren.

Last, and mostly, I was moved to tears and overcome with emotion because I remembered the prayers that Dad and I had prayed for you and Laura… prayers that a life commitment from us (Dad and I) to the two of you would help you make commitments in your own lives. Commitments like getting an education, becoming a spouse, becoming a parent, and living a Christian life. Most of my emotion was heartfelt gratitude to God for answering our prayers for you! I was so overcome with emotion that I trembled because I felt the very presence of God that day.

Dad and I can't wait to get a copy of your book and read the final version!

We love you!

Mom and Dad

Thanks, Mom and Dad, and I was honored that day to pay what you both have done for Laura and me forward and follow in your love-filled footsteps!

That night we had a lot of family come in and the McLaughlins as well, my third set of foster parents. If you go to http://raycomgroup. worldnow.com/story/31099118/fmr-foster-childs-life-comes-full-circle-after-becoming-a-foster-parent and go to the full site, you can watch a news feed WSFA did. The second couple whom they interviewed who said, "I think he is trying to pay back, I think" and "He has the heart to do that," that was Jim and Sharon McLaughlin. One other thing I remember about that adoption night was, my Pepa Oden got real emotional when he told me and my family, the first time he met and held Gabbi, he finally understood how God could love children he hasn't met yet. That was a blessing to hear him say that!

The next few days, I got several e-mails from people all over the southern half of this country, with words of thanks and encouragement. A few were particularly touching, and I wanted to share them with you, my readers. These are what they said:

First of all, let me start by saying I think opening your heart and home to your children is a wonderful thing to do. I, too, lived in many foster homes from ages six months to thirteen.

My last foster parents became my lifesaving parents. I love them every day for saving me from going back home to be abused. There are a lot of kids out there that need people like you. I have five children of my own whom I love more than anything even life itself, and I would rather die than to let them experience one ounce of my childhood. Good luck to you both as you give those precious children the happiness and safe life they so deserve. Children are born so innocent and resilient and a lot of parents take that for granted. (Elizabeth O'Neill)

Elizabeth is so right about children being born so innocent and resilient; that is one of the reasons they are so special!

Richard,

What a beautiful story this is. I know you must be so proud of your family. God has truly blessed you to get to be the Papa of those beautiful children and blessed them as well to have such a hardworking man of character to raise them. Thank you so much for sharing this part of your life with me. I am touched and honored. It is a pleasure to work with someone as fine as you. Keep up the hard work. I know there must be struggles, but you more than most know the real value.

Incredible,
Holly Judd

Holly is right too. God has truly shown me the value of hard work, and he has definitely blessed me because of it! Thank you both and many others who took the time to reach out to me and encourage me. It is a true blessing!

CHAPTER 35

Expectations

Now I want to tell you my expectations for this book. This may be brave because I have yet to see any other books address this particular topic. I, however, shoot for the stars and I am not afraid of failure when doing so. These expectations are not because I think that I am an extraordinary writer. I'll be the first one to tell you that is not the case. However, I do know my life, and if God can take my life and do what He has with it, then the sky is the limit for my book. Wouldn't you agree! I would ask you to remember what I said earlier in this book about it being God's will and not my will. If this book does not reach these expectations of mine (not God's), but they change just one *more* life (the Sgt Nick Weiers family) in any way, than this book was worth it and a huge success. I expect this book to be blessed by God and to be used as a tool to encourage others to seek and find Him and help encourage past, current, and future foster children and parents while simultaneously getting people to, as I have stated many times before, take that leap of faith with God and become foster/ adoptive parents. One thing I don't understand is that I am the only one I know who was a foster child and have become a foster parent, and I would like you, my readers, to ask the same question I have been asking for a long time now, and that question is why? If you were in foster care and you had good foster parents, why aren't you paying it forward? You know better than most that there are kids out there who need a good, loving home. If you were a foster kid and you did not have good foster parents, why aren't you doing something about it? Why not give a child, whom you could relate to better than most, a home that you felt you should have had? I could say the exact same thing for adopted children. Why am I the only one I know who was adopted and has adopted children? *Why?* I know there might be some of you out there whom I have not met yet, and if you are out there, I look forward to finding you, for I have been looking for some people like me for some time now, and I will say thank you for paying it forward. I know you are blessed, just like I am! I also expect this book to do much good—with your help, of course—for our military and foster care/adoption charities, not to mention for those who are not cut out to be foster/adoptive parents or who are not cut out to serve in our military to seek and find ways to go the extra mile and encourage and serve those fostering and in our military. I expect this book to be a best seller and get me on Fox News, on some of my favorite shows like *The O'Reilly Factor, The Kelly File* with Megyn Kelly, *The Five, The Sean Hannity Show, Justice with Judge Jeanine, Huckabee, On the Record with Greta Van Susteren*, and on any other outlets like the Today Show so I can get my message out there. I pray that this book will help people understand more of what our veterans, do indeed, sacrifice.

My dream is to have this book give me a chance to accomplish another dream of mine, and that is to become a motivational speaker.

You see, the number one reason I get from people when I ask them if they have ever thought of being a foster/adoptive parent is, and I quote, "*I* don't want to get *my* heart broken if and when the kids go back." When I hear this, I often think, what would have become of me if my foster parents, the Browns, McLaughlins, Bobos, Odens, Samples, and the rest had that same attitude? Would I have this story to tell? My answer is obviously, *no*! I would ask each and every one of you to take a deep look at the root of this reason above.

I understand your "Philistine", your fear, and know that there is a really good chance your heart will, indeed, get broken, but remember what I said—something this worthwhile will not be easy, but you will experience time with your kids that will make it all worth it, and God will bless you! If you are honest with yourself, I think you will find that this reason is selfish. There are so many good kids out there who know nothing but a bad history, who need to be shown the love of God, the affection of Him toward us, and stability. Remember MSgt Weiers and his wife's words; maybe, just maybe, you found this book, and you too can hear God calling you through this tool. I pray that is the case. Remember how I started this book, with scripture—in particular, Jeremiah 29:11—that reads, "For I know the thoughts that I think toward you, says the Lord, thoughts of peace and not of evil, to give you **a future and a hope**." I put *future* and *hope* bold there because for foster children anywhere, if someone would just give these kids a home and show them two things—what love is and who God is—they will, indeed, have a *future and a hope!* Time and again, when people hear of our story, most of the time the response is, "I could never do that." When I hear this I tell them I think God has a funny sense of humor. Let me tell you what Brittany and I could never do. For me, I could never be taken in foster care at 6 years old, move eleven different times in six years with 4 ½ of those years being in the same home, and turn out to be successful. I could never look on the past of my foster care experience and realize that God indeed had a plan for me through all the trials and turmoil in my life. For Brittany and I, we could never have three foster kids, get pregnant then I get deployed to Afghanistan where I would be when our biological daughter was born. But we did it and we did it with God. Don't limit God's power in your life or the ability to save some-one else's. I will leave you with these few words: *Let's make it about the kids and not about ourselves.* May God always bless you and keep you. Thank you all so much and amen!

Acknowledgments

First off I would like to thank each and every individual who had a hand in this book; for those who had inserts, I say thank you and well done. I did my very best not to coach anybody in what to say. I gave them all broad topics and let them write. This is why we both may have covered the same memories.

To the Tenth Street church of Christ Congregation, thank you so much for doing exactly what I asked and going the extra mile and taking care of my family while I was deployed—from babysitting, feeding them, cleaning, working the yard, and doing the laundry to saying prayers, just to name a few. Thank you! A special thank-you goes to Becky Lazenby for coming up with the idea and coordinating the sign-up list!

To my publisher, Christian Faith Publishing, thank you so much for working with me and making me feel like you really wanted this book. To Holly and Erica, you guys have been great to work with, and I say to your boss, man, they both deserve a raise!

To those who like to find every little detail of my story and fact-check it, you may find some small details, like the order in which I stayed in my foster homes and the ages. I did, by the way, say this in the book itself, but cut me some slack. I did not intentionally mislead anyone, and if you have ever been in foster care and moved around a lot—eleven times in six years, like I did—you would realize it was a whole lot to remember.

To my website developer and fellow veteran, Jonathan King, owner of DropZone Development, thank you for a job well done! Thank you and your family for yours and their service to our country!

To David Johnson, CEO of Strategic Vision PR Group, thank you so much for helping me get my story out there on a national scale. Great job!

Charities You Are Helping

Throughout this book I have told you that I will be donating a portion of all proceeds of this book to foster care/adoption and military charities; these are just a few:

1. Agape of North Alabama Inc.

This is where it all started for me. I had godly foster parents and many Christmas presents because of Agape of North Alabama.

Agape of North Alabama (www.agapecares.org) is a faith-based child-placing agency, licensed by the State of Alabama and head-quartered in Huntsville. Agape serves abused and neglected children and hurting families in the twenty-two northernmost counties of Alabama, offering birth parent counseling and adoptive services, domestic and international home study services, and traditional foster care, family reunification, and family preservation/wraparound services. Agape was founded in 1969 and is an IRS-recognized 501(c)(3) nonprofit organization; as such, all donations made to Agape are tax-deductible (www.agapecares.org/?page_id=86).

2. BigHouse Foundation in Opelika, Alabama

BigHouse has played a major role in our life as foster/adoptive parent. Micah Melnick started BigHouse. This is her story in her own words:

BigHouse is a nonprofit ministry dedicated to providing resources and building relationships with foster families. We connect the resources, generosity and unique gifts the community has to offer with the needs of children in foster care. We know not everyone is able to foster, but everyone can contribute in some way, through time, resources or prayer!

3. Together We Rise of California

I found out about Together We Rise by way of BigHouse Foundation. They partner with each other in an effort to help as many foster children as possible. I found it profound that when I came into foster care on November 17, 1988, I used one single black trash bag as my suitcase, and foster kids still used those trash bags to move twenty-eight years later.

The Story of Together We Rise

Danny Mendoza founded TWR in 2008 while still in college. For his nine-year-old cousin who was living in a car at the time, Danny reached out and did everything he could to help. However, government agencies denied him due to federal regulations. Danny always had aspirations of seeking positive change, but when he could not find a place to take him on as volunteer at a young age, Danny was left disheartened.

After telling others about his vision, Danny was inspired by encouragement from friends and colleagues to use his ambition to help others and start something himself; thus Together We Rise was born.

Together We Rise is a 501(c)(3) nonprofit organization dedicated to transforming the way youth navigate through the foster care system in America. We collaborate with community partners to bring resources to foster youth and use service-learning activities to educate volunteers on issues surrounding the system.

TWR works with hundreds of foster agencies, social workers, CASA advocates, and other partners to bring our programs to foster youth across the nation. Our foundation has allowed us to provide thousands of foster youth across the country with new bicycles, college scholarships, and suitcases so that children do not have to travel from home to home with their belongings in a trash bag.

4. The USO

I know firsthand what this military charity does. When I was in Afghanistan, I used their tent and resources numerous times!

These are just a few of the foster care/adoption and military charities you are helping with the purchase of *My Full Life Circle Squared*. If you are compelled, please give more any way you can. Thank you. —Senior Airman Richard Oden

About the Author

Senior Airman Richard Oden is a very passionate thirty-three-year-old man who resides in Opelika, Alabama, with his wife, Brittany, and their four children. Richard works as a UPS driver on the Jordan-Hare Stadium side of the Auburn University campus. He is also a member of the Alabama Air National Guard. His unit is the 187th Fighter Wing, descendants of the Tuskegee Airmen Red Tails, located at Dannelly Field in Montgomery, Alabama, as an F-16 Fighting Falcons crew chief. Richard and Brittany are active advocates for foster/adoption and military causes. Although they have adopted a sibling group of three out of foster care, they still maintain their foster care license and are currently foster parents to a newborn baby boy. Their dream is to buy a house big enough to foster sibling groups. Richard was compelled to write this book to show the world the providence of God and His will in Richard's life, for he too was a foster child, and he too was adopted out of foster care. Richard is also very passionate about the US military—so much so he joined it when he was twenty-eight years old. He and his family are also active members of Tenth Street church of Christ in Opelika, Alabama.